COASTLINE

Catalans call them *seitons* (say-tons), Provençals call them *anchois* (ansh-wa), Ligurians call them *acciughe* (achoo-geh). For 4000 years anchovies have been a core ingredient in the cuisine of the sun.

COASTLINE

The food of Mediterranean
Italy, France & Spain

Lucio Galletto
& David Dale

murdoch books

Sydney | London

Contents

About the authors

LUCIO GALLETTO

Lucio Galletto was born on the border of Liguria and Tuscany in north-western Italy, where his family had opened a restaurant in the fishing village of Bocca di Magra. He was working as a waiter there and studying architecture when he fell in love with a passing Australian backpacker and decided to move to Sydney. Over three decades, his art-filled restaurant, Lucio's, has won numerous awards, and in 2008 he received the Medal of the Order of Australia for 'service to the community through contributions as a restaurateur and author, and to the support of arts organisations'. His books include *The Art of Traditional Italian*; and, co-written with David Dale, *The Art of Pasta*, *Lucio's Ligurian Kitchen* and *Soffritto: A Delicious Ligurian Memoir*.

DAVID DALE

David Dale is a writer and broadcaster on travel, food, popular culture and anthropology. He trained as a psychologist but decided he would do less harm to the cause of mental health if he went into journalism. He has been a reporter, feature writer, foreign correspondent and editor for all of Australia's major media organisations and his 14 books include *Anatolia: Adventures in Turkish Cooking*; *The 100 Things Everyone Needs to Know about Italy*; *Essential Places: A book about ideas and where they started*; *The Little Book of Australia*; and *The Obsessive Traveller: Or why I don't steal towels from great hotels any more*. He teaches journalism at The University of Technology, Sydney.

COLLIOURE (FRENCH CATALUNYA): The lanes near the beach are lined with tiny food shops.

David's introduction

When I suggested this project to Lucio Galletto, he reflected for a couple of seconds and said: 'Yes, that should be okay. Paella is just burnt risotto, isn't it?'

He was joking, of course, as he often is. He might equally have said 'Bouillabaisse is just *zuppa di pesce* with toast on top', or 'Ratatouille is just undercooked *samfaina*', or '*Pistou* is just pesto without cheese'. He got my notion immediately — that the various cuisines of the western Mediterranean are really branches of a single olive tree that was planted 2600 years ago by the Greeks, and fertilised by the Romans and the Arabs, and we ought to get a useful book out of exploring how the cuisines overlap. At the very least, it was a great excuse for a road trip through some of Europe's liveliest cooking, warmest communities and most spectacular seascapes.

All Lucio would have to do was construct a bunch of recipes based on our experiences in Catalunya, Provence and Liguria, while I gathered the stories and tasted the food. Lucio was amused by my theory that, as a descendant of the Liguri tribe which once controlled the coastline between what is now Barcelona and what is now Carrara, he was in a unique position to help me chronicle how his tribe's eating habits have evolved over three millennia.

This book had been germinating in my head for about 30 years, ever since I read a remark by the American food scholar Waverley Root in *The Food of France*. Root said the national boundaries within modern Europe make no sense: they force disparate peoples into artificial alliances and split once cohesive cultures along borders created by accidents of war and diplomacy. He suggested it would be more logical to segregate Europeans by their preferred cooking medium: into The Domain of Butter, The Domain of Lard and The Domain of Olive Oil. The Domain of Butter would include most of France, Belgium, Switzerland and the Netherlands. The Domain of Lard would include most of Germany, Scandinavia, the nations that used to be Yugoslavia, and a pocket of north-eastern Italy. The Domain of Oil would include southern France, most of Spain, and most of Italy and Greece.

Since I embraced the logic of Root's new European borders, most of my travelling, cooking and eating has been through The Domain of Oil. It became apparent that the citizens of Valencia (Spain) have more in common with the citizens of Collioure (France) than with the citizens of Madrid; the residents of the Cinque Terre (Italy) have more in common with the residents of Nice (France) than with the residents of Rome; and the Marseillais have more in common with Catalans and Ligurians than with Parisians, despite having a national anthem named after them.

My deeper understanding of The Domain of Oil began in 2001, when I was in eastern Liguria researching a book (called *Soffritto*) about the area where Lucio grew up. In 1950, Lucio's father and uncle built a shack on a beach where the Magra River enters the sea, and started serving *zuppa di pesce* (fish stew) to the locals. They didn't know it, but they were replicating the behaviour of a bunch of Greek mariners who had bumped onto that shore 2600 years earlier.

Lucio grew up between the tables of the family restaurant, Capannina Ciccio, but at the age of 23 fell in love with an Australian backpacker and moved to Sydney, where he now runs one of

Australia's most awarded Italian restaurants. His cousin Mario still runs Capannina Ciccio, and still serves *zuppa di pesce* where the Magra enters the sea on the border of Tuscany and Liguria.

A few minutes' drive from Mario's place are the ruins of a Roman city called Luni. One morning, while Lucio and I were examining the ancient amphitheatre, we met a tour guide named Sara, who told us that 2000 years ago, this had been a marble city so magnificent that invading barbarians thought it was Rome. Although Luni is three kilometres inland nowadays, it was then a deep bay, described by the geographer Strabo in 10 AD as 'just such a place as would become the naval base of a people who were masters of so great a sea for so long a time', meaning the Romans.

Sara said she hated the Romans for what they had done to 'her people' — the Liguri tribe, who had been subjected to 'ethnic cleansing'. Sara told us the Romans had launched the invasion of Hispania from their naval base at Luni, and had presumably done the same sort of ethnic cleansing on the Hispanics who had, up to then, lived harmoniously with the Greeks who set up trading posts on the Spanish shoreline.

Some 15 years later, at the end of my travels for this book, I was standing where the Romans from Luni landed — the beach of Tarragona in central Catalunya. Tarragona is famous nowadays not only for its Roman ruins, but for its paella (using rice brought by the Arabs) and its *fideua* (using dry pasta, also brought by the Arabs).

So this is a book about how they eat in The Domain of Oil, which owes its existence to the adventurousness of Greek mariners nearly 3000 years ago, the determination of Roman empire builders 2000 years ago, and the ingenuity of Arab traders 1000 years ago. It's also a book about the pleasure of sharing, and how societies that sometimes seem divided are actually united in the details of life that really matter.

– David Dale

CASSIS (PROVENCE):
The fishing village is a
weekend retreat for the
citizens of Marseille.

RECCO (LIGURIA):
The town specialty,
cheese-stuffed focaccia,
needs a generous drizzle
of Ligurian olive oil
before it goes in the
wood-fired oven.

Chapter One

ORIGINI ED ESSENZIALI / ORIGINES ET DETAILS /
ORIGENS I FONAMENTS

Origins & Essentials

CAMOGLI (LIGURIA):
The town still depends
on its fishing industry.

In the beginning

Before we start this voyage, there are two and a half words of ancient Greek you need to know: kakavi, kakavia *and* emporion.

kakavi is a three-legged cooking pot designed to stand over a small fire. That word extended to *kakavia*, which means a kind of fish stew that could be simmered in that pot. The Greeks' *kakavia* became *zuppa di pesce* in Italy, *sarsuela* in Spain and *bouillabaisse* in France, but we'll get to them later.

The last word you'll need is *emporion* — a trading post or shopping centre set up by Greek mariners to sell pots to astonished locals on the coast of what is now Catalunya, Provence and Liguria. Through their emporions, the Greeks spread olive oil, fish stew and civilisation around the Mediterranean.

Now we can begin. Cast your mind back 2700 years to the busy Aegean Sea between what is now Greece and what is now Turkey. The Trojan War is over, and the Greeks are wondering how they can build their economy. They have found so many uses for the produce of their olive trees — medicine (rubbed on skin rashes, swallowed to ease constipation); perfume; lubricant; fuel for lamps; anointing fluid in religious rituals; dressing for salads; and a cooking medium lighter than animal fats — they're wondering if other people around the Mediterranean might consider them worth buying. Their sales pitch will include how olive oil was a gift from the goddess Athena, whose name was then attached to the biggest Greek city.

So they set off in their galleys, powered by a single sail and 30 slaves (15 oars per side), and glide past the bottom of the Greek mainland and the bottom of the Italian mainland.

They land in the north-east of Spain, the south of France and the north-west of Italy, bringing their pots, olive tree seedlings, a good supply of saffron, and a recipe for fish stew. They build fences around their emporions and proceed to cook the fish they've caught, flavouring the water with saffron. Then they start to trade with the locals.

They throw the guts of all the fish they've eaten into tanks with a lot of salt and make a sauce which comes to be called *garum,* and which becomes an addiction with the Romans who start arriving 300 years later.

The Romans admire the Greeks and want to trade with them, so instead of taking over the emporions, they build towns near them and help them to subdue an annoying local tribe called the Liguri.

The Greeks are happy to let the Romans push roads through their land, so they can spread their empire through France to Spain.

The Romans extend the olive groves throughout their empire and augment the local fish-and-saffron diet with their own culinary favourites — ham, figs, chickpeas, lentils, thyme, rosemary, fava beans, apples and pears. The two cultures live in harmony until 49 BC, when the Greeks in Massilia and in Empúries make a political mistake. In the civil war that breaks out across the empire, they side with General Pompey in his war against an upstart called Julius Caesar. Pompey loses, and so do the Greeks, and their emporions are absorbed into Caesar's empire.

As the Romans fade away 400 years later, the coastline is overrun from the north by raiding and trading Vikings, Visigoths, Vandals, Huns and assorted barbarians (so-called because they have beards — *barbe* — which looked untidy to the Romans). All of them leave their influences on local cuisine, and all of them leave. Then, from the south, come the Arabs, who settle in and start to cook with rice, dry pasta, eggplants (aubergines), oranges, sugar, and various nuts that were known to the Romans but considered too exotic for everyday consumption.

The Arabs control north-western Spain for 50 years, but are driven back to the south by Christian warriors, who then proceed to fight amongst themselves for control of areas they come to call Catalunya, Provence and Liguria.

And so we reach the present day, when fragments of the coastline have been given publicity-seeking nicknames such as (west to east) Costa Daurada (Golden Coast), Costa Brava (Wild Coast), Côte Vermeille (Vermillion Coast), Côte d'Azur (Blue Coast), Riviera di Ponente (Coast of the Setting Sun) and Riviera di Levante (Coast of the Rising Sun).

All these coasts are linked by a shared history and a shared love of one cooking medium: olive oil.

In researching this book, we set off in search of similarities, and we had no trouble finding them. That's why so many of the recipes in this book have two or even three titles. If some of the names look unusual, that's because we've used the Catalan language rather than Castillian Spanish (thus *patates braves*, not *patatas bravas*), occasionally the Provençal or Niçois dialect rather than Parisian French (thus *pissaladiera*, not *pissaladière*), and occasionally Ligurian dialect rather than standard Florentine Italian. We've tried to give due credit if a dish seemed to originate in one part of the coastline and then spread east or west.

But let's not get ahead of ourselves. We need to maintain a little suspense. We want you to read the stories of the coastline before you start your cooking adventures, letting the fascinating facts and fables slowly unfold so you absorb the spirit of the place. We want you to go there and experience our journey for yourself, so we've concluded this book with some suggestions on where to eat, between the Roman amphitheatre in eastern Liguria on the river Magra, and the Roman amphitheatre in southern Catalunya, overlooking the beach at Tarragona.

Let's start with some practical advice on what you'll be cooking, and how you can make the most of it.

LUNI (LIGURIA): The Roman amphitheatre could hold a crowd of 7000.

A few favourite ingredients

ALMONDS are huge in Catalan cooking, a craze introduced by the Romans and reinforced by the Arabs. They are less popular in Provence and rarely used in Liguria. Spain is the world's third biggest grower of almonds (after the United States and Australia), but can reasonably claim to have the world's best — particularly the type called marcona, grown just south of Tarragona. The recipes in this book mostly use blanched almonds, but if you have whole ones, put them in boiling water for a minute, rinse in cold water and then peel by rubbing them between your fingers to push the skin off. To enhance their flavour, we suggest you dry the almonds and toast them for 3 minutes in an oven preheated to 200ºC (400ºF). You can do the same with walnuts and hazelnuts, the other nutty delights of the coastline.

ANCHOVIES swim all around the Med coastline, but they are best when caught off Collioure in France, the Cinque Terre in Liguria and the Costa Brava in Catalunya. The locals will tell you the technique for preserving them in salt was brought to this shore by the Greeks. The taste of mashed anchovies is the nearest modern humans are going to get to the taste of *garum*, the sauce created by the Greeks and spread round the Mediterranean by the Romans.

The difference between white anchovies (sold at gourmet delis) and brown anchovies (sold in jars or tins at the supermarket) is simply that the white fillets have been marinated in vinegar, while the brown ones have been preserved in salt and then covered in oil. The white ones tend to be used in tapas because they look better, but the brown ones can be excellent.

The best tinned anchovies are not full of bones and not salty, and are sold in extra virgin olive oil (put them in the fridge — if the oil solidifies, it's a good one; if it doesn't, change the oil). You can make your own improvement to cheap anchovies. Drain them of whatever medium they are in, place them in a bowl, cover them with a mixture of the best olive oil, a little finely chopped garlic, a squeeze of lemon, half a teaspoon of white wine vinegar and a tablespoon of finely chopped parsley (or basil, if you want a stronger flavour). Let them marinate for at least half an hour before putting them on toast.

ARTICHOKES may seem like a waste of money, since you have to throw away more than half of any fresh artichoke you buy, but we reckon they are worth the trouble. Pull off most of the outer leaves, cut off the top half of the remaining leaves, scoop out the beard, and then, to ensure they don't go black, leave them in a lot of water with the juice of half a lemon until you are ready to cook with them.

Bear in mind that there is no point in drinking a fine wine with artichokes, as they neutralise the flavour of the wine in your mouth.

AUBERGINES *see* eggplants.

BACCALA (salt cod) was spread around the Med by Vikings. The name is supposedly from the Latin *baculum*, a walking stick, because the salted cod from Norway was sold in sticks (the air-dried version is called *stoccafisso*, literally 'stickfish'). If you can buy it cleaned and deboned, as you can in the Boqueria market in Barcelona, lucky you. More likely you will find it in salty bony chunks. You'll need to soak it for 48 hours, changing the water three or four times a day. Then bring a pot of water to the boil, turn off the heat, and put the salt cod in the water for 10 minutes to soften it so you can remove the bones and skin. At this point it is pretty smelly.

The Provençals mix it with mashed potato and call it *brandade de morue*. The Ligurians poach it for 15 minutes with a bay leaf, put it in a deep serving bowl and dress it with a pesto of parsley, capers, garlic, pine nuts and olive oil. They let it rest for at least 2 hours and serve it with hot toast as an appetiser.

BASIL in this book is only ever sweet basil (with round, light green leaves, not thin minty-looking leaves), and we think the best way to make *Pesto alla Genovese* (page 30) is with the smallest leaves in the bunch. If you're stuck with big leaves, be sure to remove the centre stems, because they will embitter your sauce. If you're cooking with basil, put it in the stew or soup at the end of the simmering process, to retain its flavour.

BEANS come in many shapes, sizes and colours, but our favourites are fava, cannellini and what Italians call *bianchi di Spagna* (literally 'whites of Spain', which are also called butter or lima beans). Fava beans, also known as broad beans, are great in spring, when they can be eaten raw (if very young or double-peeled), just dressed with extra virgin olive oil, salt and pepper. Cannellini and lima beans can be used with the Catalan peasant treat called *botifarra amb mongetes* — beans in tomato sofregit stewed with grilled pork sausages. They're also excellent in a salad with tinned tuna, sliced red onions and olive oil.

We're not keen on tinned beans, because they tend to be soft and slimy. If you can't find fresh, soak the dried ones overnight, change the water, and boil them for 30 minutes with bay leaves and a few chunks of carrot and celery.

BREAD in this book is focaccia you make yourself (see page 174), or toasted slices of French-style baguette (for the little rafts that float on fish soup), or toasted slices of Italian-style ciabatta (to be tastily topped for crostini, or to be rubbed with garlic and tomato for our *Pa amb tomaquet* on page 70). For thickening sauces, we use the soft inside of any bread except supermarket sliced.

CAPERS, another gift of the Greeks, should be the small Italian variety, bought dry in salt, not wet in vinegar. Wash off the salt before using them.

CHARD is an ancient green also called silverbeet in English (or *blette* in French or *bietole* in Italian), and sometimes strangely prefaced with the word 'Swiss'. Treat it as a tougher version of spinach.

CHICKPEAS were taken to Hispania by the Romans and embraced all around the Mediterranean, often as an alternative to wheat. The tinned versions are okay, but we prefer to soak dried ones overnight, change the water and then boil them with bay leaves, carrot and celery for about an hour. For the pancake called *socca* in Nice and *farinata* in Genoa (see page 189), we use a chickpea flour called besan, but you should try to find the European version, because the Indian version does not work so well.

EGGPLANTS (aubergines) seem to have originated in India, and were spread around the Mediterranean by the Arabs at least 1000 years ago. They are popular in Catalan and Provençal cooking (you couldn't make *samfaina* or *ratatouille* without them; see page 74), but the Ligurians tend to look upon them as a weird Sicilian invader. In our recipes we prefer to use the long slim eggplants (sometimes called 'Japanese' eggplants) rather than the giant spongy ones often found in supermarkets. Remember they need to be cooked for longer than their cousins, the zucchini (courgettes), so put them in your stew immediately after the onions.

FIGS were first cultivated in eastern Anatolia (the Kurdish part of modern Turkey) about 8000 years ago, and were favourites of both Greeks and Romans at all stages of a meal. In early autumn, they are the perfect companion to Spanish ham or Italian prosciutto. You don't need a recipe.

GARLIC is the flavouring used most often in this book, mashed raw into sauces, or fried for stews and soups. To avoid bitterness, you should put the peeled chopped garlic in lukewarm olive oil and bring it slowly up to a sizzle, then take it off (or add the next ingredients) after only 2 minutes, when the garlic should have turned golden.

HERBS such as rosemary, thyme or oregano are fresh leaves plucked from the stalk, like the Romans would have done, rather than any dried version. And when we say parsley, we always mean the flat-leaf European kind, not the boring crinkly type the British sometimes use; it's best finely chopped and sprinkled on a stew just before serving.

We use dried herbs mostly in the form of Herbes de Provence, a mixture that became an international fad in the 1970s. You can make your own by mixing 1 tablespoon each of dried thyme, basil, marjoram and rosemary with half a tablespoon each of fennel seeds and dried oregano. You get more flavour if you crush the herbs and seeds together in a mortar before adding them to a stew. Sometimes the Provençals also throw in a bouquet garni, which is a bundle of fresh and dried herbs tied together with string or in a little muslin (cheesecloth) bag. The most common elements of a bouquet garni are thyme, rosemary and bay leaves. Dried strips of orange rind can give it zing.

OLIVE OIL in this book ALWAYS means extra virgin, whether for cooking or dressing, so buy a four litre (one gallon) tin and keep it near the stove to be splashed into the pan whenever a recipe specifies. For deep-frying, we suggest a cheaper vegetable oil such as sunflower or canola.

OLIVES in Provence and Liguria are mostly the small black variety, sometimes called Niçoise or Taggiasca. To remove the stones, cut off the tip of the olive and squash it with the flat of a carving knife, then cut down one side and pull out the pip.

ONIONS need to be fried for much longer than garlic, to reach their ideal sweetness, so put them in the oil first, over medium heat, and start adding other ingredients after at least 5 minutes. If you want them raw in a salad, we suggest using red ones (sometimes called 'Spanish' onions). For cooking, we think brown onions taste better.

PASTA in this book is both fresh (made at home, usually with eggs, and needing to be boiled for only a couple of minutes) and dry (bought in packets, and needing to be boiled for at least 8 minutes, depending on how *al dente* or chewy you like it). The Catalans' preferred form of dry pasta is called *fideus*, which is hard to find outside of Spain. We suggest you break up spaghettini or vermicelli.

PEPPERS such as chillies and capsicums (called bell peppers in

America) arrived in Europe (from the Americas) in the 16th century, and were embraced first in Spain. The Ligurians still haven't fully accepted them.

To skin a capsicum, you need to burn the outside until it's blistered and black (on a barbecue, under a grill/broiler, at the top of an oven at maximum temperature, or on a gas hob), then let it cool, slice it in half, and remove the stalk, membranes and the seeds. In southern France, a favourite appetiser involves skinning red, green and yellow capsicums in that way, slicing them into strips and laying out alternating colours on a platter, topped with anchovies. We ate that in Nice, Cassis, Sète and Collioure and it came to define the colours of this part of the Med.

PAPRIKA is made from dried capsicums (bell peppers) and, under the name *pimentón*, is an essential flavouring for paella. We mostly use smoked paprika or sweet paprika in our recipes.

RICE for paella should have short, fat grains; an ideal form is Calasparra. Don't try to use the Arborio-style rice you've bought for risotto, which is likely to have longer grains, and is designed to give a creamy texture you do not want in paella.

SAFFRON was thought to be a relaxant by the Greeks, who enjoyed the legend that their *kakavia* (saffron and seafood soup) was invented by Aphrodite (Venus) to put her husband Hephaestus (Vulcan) to sleep while she had a fling with Aries (Mars). Buy saffron threads, not powder. To bring up the flavour, toss the threads in a dry frying pan over high heat for about 30 seconds. Add them towards the end of your stewing process. A little saffron goes a long way.

SEAFOOD has different names all around the world, and we've tried to give lots of options in our recipes. The Greeks who started the Mediterranean repertoire baked big beautiful fish whole for their banquets, and chopped up small ugly fish for their stews, simmering the firm-fleshed ones for a few minutes longer than the fragile-fleshed ones — a tradition still followed around the coastline. Ligurians are obsessed with mussels, and like to add them to seafood stews, while the Marseillais say shellfish have no place in *Bouillabaisse* (page 196), and should be served separately. Whatever you do with mussels and clams (vongole), make sure to keep the liquid they expel when heated. It makes a delicious stock.

STOCKS are not much used in Ligurian cooking, but essential in French and Catalan cooking. We won't complain if you shortcut our recipes by buying a good commercial chicken stock or seafood stock, but you'll find more flavour and authenticity by using the following.

For chicken stock, throw a lot of chicken bones (drumsticks are best) into a big pot with 3 bay leaves and 1 roughly chopped carrot, onion, celery stalk and leek. Fill with water to the top, bring the water to the boil, then simmer uncovered for 1 hour, and covered for 2 hours more. Skim the top and pass the liquid through a fine strainer. You can keep the stock in the fridge for a week, or in the freezer for up to 6 months.

For a basic fish stock, you'll need a lot of fish heads and bones (the leftovers from making our *Bouillabaisse* on page 196, for example). Thoroughly wash the fish bits, then fry them in olive oil over medium heat for about 5 minutes, squashing the bits down to extract the juices. Throw in a quarter cup of white wine and let the alcohol evaporate for 3 minutes. Now throw in a roughly chopped carrot, celery stalk, onion and leek, fill to the top with water, and simmer for at least 30 minutes. Push the mixture through a fine strainer. You can keep the stock in the fridge for 3 days, or in the freezer for up to 6 months.

MARSEILLE (PROVENCE):
In the market, always check
the produce for freshness.

TOMATOES should be skinned and seeded before you cook with them, because we don't like the look of skins floating around or the bitterness sometimes contributed by the seeds. The best way to skin a tomato is to carve a cross in its bottom and place it in boiling water for about a minute, then plunge it into iced water. Some say you can get the same effect by carving the cross and putting the tomato (covered) in a microwave at full power for 30 seconds. In some of our recipes, we refer to 'tomatoes, grated to the skin'. This is a fun process which involves slicing a tomato in half, then pushing one half up and down on a grater over bread until just before the point when your palm bleeds.

WINES used to be mixed with honey and water in Greek and Roman times, but these days, that would be sacrilege. You could follow these broad principles: before a meal, drink Cava, the sparkling wine of Catalunya; with Provençal seafood, drink a golden Rosé; with Ligurian seafood, drink Vermentino; with spicy Catalan dishes, drink the big reds Monastrell and Tempranillo, first planted by the Romans near Tarragona; with desserts, drink Muscat de Rivesaltes or Banyuls from near Collioure.

A NOTE ON QUANTITIES

Most of the recipes here are hundreds or even thousands of years old, developed long before people had measuring tools beyond their hands, eyes, and noses.

Although we have tried to give reasonably precise measurements, we're not fussy about them. Feel free to interpret our advice according to your taste and to experiment with our basic outlines. Nobody's going to be poisoned by a handful more or less of basil, a splash more or less of olive oil, a grind more or less of black pepper. In our view, there is no such thing as too much garlic, while we tend to be restrained in our use of chilli. An avalanche of saffron is not necessarily a good way to flavour a stew, and it's pretty expensive, but if it makes you feel aligned with the ancient Greeks, go for it.

KITCHEN EQUIPMENT is one thing you need to consider. If you're in the habit of cooking at home, you already have the pans, bowls, carving knives, wooden spoons, chopping boards and baking tins we mention in our recipes.

A paella pan and a pizza tray will ensure authenticity.

Terracotta cooking pots and a big mortar and pestle would be desirable if you want to time-travel, but an electric blender and a couple of heavy-based frying pans will get you by.

An olive pitter would be handy for cherries as well as olives, and a piping (icing) bag and nozzle will let you be ambitious with desserts.

And large serving platters and bowls to go in the middle of the table are vital for the many sharing dishes you're about to encounter.

GENOA (LIGURIA): The city is full of *salumerias* for those who don't have time to make their own sauces.

Chapter Two

SALSE / SAUCES / SALSES

Sauces & Dips

CINQUE TERRE (LIGURIA): The cliffs have been draped with grapevines for centuries, but the winemakers now use a monorail instead of donkeys to bring the baskets of grapes uphill.

Back to the grindstone

The Ligurian word pesto, *the Provençal word* pistou,
and the Catalan word pisto *all come from the Latin verb*
pestare, *which means to pound or crush.*

So does the English word *pestle*. This is a chapter crammed with pestos, which we hope you will make with a pestle rather than a blender, a word which has no Mediterranean origin.

The first recorded pesto was a sauce called *moretum*, described in a collection of poems called *Appendix Vergiliana*, circulated in Rome during the 1st century. Here's a rough translation of the recipe, which begins with a peasant named Symilus making a paste for his bread. He picks up four cloves of garlic and some parsley, rue, celery and coriander. Then he puts the garlic into a mortar:

'*He sprinkles grains of salt, and cheese, hard from taking up the salt. The herbs he now introduces and he breaks the reeking garlic with the pestle, then rubs everything in the mingled juice. His hand moves in circles until by degrees the ingredients lose their own powers, and out of many comes a single colour, not entirely green nor white from the cheese because that colour is altered by so many herbs. The vapour assails the man's uncovered nostrils.*'

We hope you will share that experience with Symilus, using your mortar as a time machine and returning to the days when a bit of physical exertion was all it took to transform ingredients. We want you to experience the warm glow in the shoulders and the tingling in the nose that Symilus enjoyed before he filled his belly every day.

That recipe for *moretum* makes no reference to olive oil, presumably because that would have been obvious to any Roman reader. What we now call extra virgin oil was a staple of Greek and Roman life, used as perfume, as fuel for lamps, and as medicine (both externally and internally), as well as a way to smooth the sauces they were pounding. It helped to spread the world's first food technology (pounding) all around the Mediterranean.

This book is about the shared approach of three great cooking cultures, but having pounded their *pesti* or simmered their salsas, the Catalans, the Ligurians and the Provençals use them differently. The Ligurians like to dollop sauces on pasta (or sometimes sauté pasta in them). The Catalans stir them into dishes such as stews and paellas to boost flavour. And the Provençals like to dip bread into them.

This chapter allows for all three uses, and for crossovers. We've suggested you base your Provençal sauce on a Catalan *sofregit*. We've suggested romesco as a topping for crostini. And we reckon aïoli (or *allioli* or *agliata*) enriches just about everything.

But remember — however fine these sauces taste when made in a blender, taking the time to pound them in a mortar will make you a better person.

Pesto alla Genovese

Around Genoa, pesto lovers call the essential ingredients of their favourite sauce 'the seven dwarves' (which presumably means Snow White is the pasta they serve it on). The dwarves are basil (small leaves, no stalks); salt; garlic (fresh, Mediterranean); pine nuts (small and raw, never roasted); olive oil (extra virgin, ideally from Liguria); pecorino (sheep's cheese, hopefully from Sardinia); and parmesan (two years old, ideally).

The recipe varies all over Liguria, particularly with the amount of garlic, and the quantity and sharpness of the two cheeses. We are suggesting the version made in the Riviera di Levante, to the east of Genoa, which we consider has the best harmony of ingredients.

Some silly writers suggest blanching the basil leaves in boiling water, in order to brighten the green colour, but we think the salt does that enough. Other silly writers suggest roasting the pine nuts, but that prevents you from making a smooth paste. Pesto should be a raw sauce, and should never be heated (only warmed, to push out its fragrance, when it is tossed through pasta off the heat).

The quantities in this recipe would make enough to serve as a sauce on pasta for four people. If you double the quantities, you can store the sauce, covered with a layer of olive oil, in a sealed jar in the fridge for up to a month.

---

90 g (3¼ oz/3 cups) small basil leaves (about 50 leaves)
1 garlic clove
a pinch of sea salt

1 tablespoon raw pine nuts
2 tablespoons freshly grated parmesan cheese

1 tablespoon freshly grated mild pecorino cheese
60 ml (2 fl oz/¼ cup) olive oil, approximately

Wash the basil leaves and dry them gently with paper towels, being careful not to squash or break them, so they don't become black and make the pesto taste bitter. Place the garlic and salt in a mortar and start crushing with the pestle.

When the garlic is crushed, add the basil leaves and continue crushing, using a rotary motion, sprinkling in a bit more sea salt to help the crushing. When the basil has 'let out its green soul' (as the Ligurians say), add the pine nuts, keep pounding for another minute, then finally add the two cheeses and a little of the olive oil. When you have a paste, transfer the mixture to a bowl and stir the remaining olive oil through.

If you insist on using a blender, put in all the ingredients and pulse slowly, to ensure the basil doesn't get hot.

Trofie al pesto

Our favourite use of pesto is to dress a vegetarian masterpiece which combines pasta, potatoes and green beans. Around Genoa, the pasta most commonly used in this dish is *trenette,* a kind of square spaghetti. Trenette may be hard to find outside Liguria, so you could substitute linguine with no loss of flavour. Or you could make your own pasta in shapes called *trofie,* which are essentially pinches of dough rubbed between your palms to take on a squiggly shape. Making trofie is good exercise for the arm muscles — first in the kneading, then in the rubbing.

*1 large waxy (boiling)
   potato
300 g (10½ oz) green
   beans
400 g (14 oz) linguine
   or trofie*

*200 ml (7 fl oz) Pesto
   sauce (see page 30)
freshly grated parmesan
   cheese, to serve*

*If making your own trofie
400 g (14 oz/2⅔ cups)
   plain (all-purpose)
   flour
a pinch of salt
4 tablespoons water*

First make the trofie. Put the flour in a bowl, sprinkle on a little salt, add the water and mix together to form a dough. Knead well until the dough is smooth and firm, adding more water if it seems dry. Let the dough rest for 30 minutes.

When you're ready to make the trofie, pinch off a small piece of the dough and rub it quickly between your palms to form the classic trofie twist shape. This may take a little practice, but it doesn't need to look perfect to taste good.

Keep doing this until you have used up all the dough. Leave the trofie to dry on a floured tea towel while you make the pesto.

Peel the potato and cut it into 1 cm (½ inch) cubes. Top and tail the beans, then slice them in half lengthways, or push them through a bean stringer.

Fill a large saucepan with water, bring it to the boil and add some salt. Drop in the potato cubes and boil for 3 minutes. If you are using linguine, add them and the beans now and boil according to the packet instructions (usually 8–10 minutes, depending on how *al dente* you like your pasta).

If you are using hand-made trofie, boil the potatoes for 5 minutes before adding the beans, then in another 3 minutes add the hand made-trofie and boil for 3 minutes more. (You can buy excellent commercially made trofie, but they will take longer to cook, so adjust times accordingly.)

Place a big dollop of pesto in a large serving bowl. Add a little of the cooking water to loosen it. Drain the pasta, beans and potato and add them to the bowl. Toss gently. Top with the rest of the pesto, toss again, sprinkle with parmesan and serve.

Basil Madness on the Med

This was the experiment, conducted in 2014: at the same time on the same day, basil seeds were planted in soil all over the Mediterranean, from Spain across to Israel (and even in Holland). A few weeks later, the leaves were analysed in a laboratory in Genoa. The result, according to the Genoa Pesto Consortium, was that the basil grown in greenhouses just north of the seaside town of Varazze (which is a little to the west of Genoa) was the best in the world — sweeter and richer in essential oils than any of the others.

Well, they would say that. The basil growers of western Liguria are fighting to have the sauce made from *their* leaves given a special trademark protection, so companies around the world cannot use the term *pesto Genovese* for products made with any oil other than olive, any nut other than pine, any cheeses other than parmesan and pecorino — and any leaf that isn't from one of the 42 million basil plants grown each year in Liguria. Already the basil of the Prà area is protected by 'Denomination of Origin' laws, but they're in search of a more powerful protection.

You'd assume from all this that pesto alla Genovese is an ancient recipe. After all, basil did originate in India, and Greek writers mentioned it 3000 years ago — around the time they were visiting the domain of the Liguri tribe.

The Genoese enjoy the notion that their most famous sailor, Cristoforo Colombo, carried spaghetti and basil plants on his voyages to the New World, and — just before discovering the tomato — was able to serve his crew nourishing meals of *pasta con pesto*. In reality, the first known recipe for the basil sauce we love today appeared in a book called *La Cuciniera Genovese*, published in 1863, and the local fanaticism only began in the 1970s.

You can enjoy pesto in almost every restaurant of Genoa; we recommend a place called Il Genovese, run by Roberto Panizza, one of the founders of the 'Fine Palates Association' that conducts a pesto-pounding competition every two years. But we urge you to venture a few kilometres east of Genoa to the town of Camogli, and try the trofie with pesto at Pasta Fresca Fiorella on the waterfront.

Camogli literally means 'house of wives', a reference to the women left behind when the local fishermen set off to work for weeks at a time. The houses along the shoreline are painted in colours bright enough for the fishermen to recognise their homes from far out to sea. A couple of streets inland, you find masterpieces of Ligurian *trompe l'oeil* — three-storey houses with blank façades upon which have been painted balconies, pediments, shutters, washing lines, even cats on windowsills in impeccably deceptive 3D. It's worth a walk through Camogli to see them, after your pesto-powered lunch.

PRÀ (LIGURIA): The farms produce basil that makes the world's finest pesto.

Pistou

When the people of Nice say *pistou*, they are often referring to their favourite summer soup (full name: *soupe au pistou*), which is a kind of minestrone seasoned with basil. Here we are talking about the classic Provençal sauce made with garlic, basil and olive oil, very similar to the *Pesto alla Genovese* (page 30) from which it derives, but much lighter because it leaves out the pine nuts and the cheeses. It's ideal for summer, when we celebrate fresh aromatic herbs, of which basil is king. Sometimes these days the French thicken their pistou with a grated hard cheese such as gruyère.

3 garlic cloves
sea salt

60 small, very fresh basil leaves
80 ml (2½ fl oz/⅓ cup) olive oil

1 tablespoon grated gruyère cheese (optional)

Place the garlic cloves in a mortar with three pinches of sea salt. Start pounding until the garlic is thoroughly crushed. Add the basil leaves and pound them against the sides of the mortar in a rotary motion, until you obtain a smooth paste. Add the olive oil slowly, drop by drop, and stir it in with the pestle.

Transfer the paste to a bowl; if the consistency seems too thick, stir in more olive oil. If you like cheese, mix the gruyère in thoroughly.

The pistou is best used straight away, but will keep in an airtight jar in the fridge for up to 3 days, as long as the sauce is covered with olive oil.

Best with: This sauce is wonderful in an omelette. Break 4 eggs into a large bowl, add a tablespoon of water and whisk until foaming. Add the pistou and whisk some more. Season with salt and pepper to taste — much more pepper than salt would be nice. Heat 3 tablespoons olive oil and 1 teaspoon butter in a large non-stick frying pan over medium heat; when the butter starts to foam, pour in the egg mixture, tilting the pan to cover the entire surface. Grate parmesan cheese on top, cover the pan and cook for a further 4 minutes. Remove from the heat and, using a spatula or two, roll the omelette from one side to the other, making a long cylinder. Place on a board, cut into segments and serve with a tomato and basil salad, or a green leaf salad. This is perfect as a starter or part of a tapas.

Mainly, however, it's essential in *soupe au pistou*, which is a kind of runny ratatouille. Some recipes include cannellini or borlotti beans, but we think they make the soup too heavy for summer, so we just boil together diced onions, carrots, celery stalks (and leaves), zucchini (courgettes), potatoes, peas, green beans and tomatoes. After simmering for 15 minutes, you can add a tiny pasta shape called *ditalini*, and boil for another 8 minutes. Divide into bowls and dollop a tablespoon of pistou into each.

That's essentially the soup that was served, during the 19th and early 20th century, to sailors passing through the port of Genoa after they'd been at sea for weeks without access to fresh vegetables. Little boats called *catrai* (floating osterias, really) would row past the ships and hand tin bowls of minestrone flavoured with pesto up to the crew, charging just a couple of lira to protect the sailors from vitamin-deficiency diseases.

EMPÚRIES (CATALUNYA): Amongst the remains of the first *emporion*, or trading post, on the Spanish coast are the tanks in which Greek settlers made the fish sauce that became an addiction across the Roman empire.

Salsa verde

Supposedly, this cold condiment for meats was brought back to Italy by Roman legionnaires who had found it in Turkey around 100 BC. It's best known as an accompaniment for that great northern Italian dish *bollito misto* (poached beef, chicken, sausage and tongue), but in Liguria we sometimes spread it on crostini, or enjoy it with meaty fish such as grilled tuna.

Here's one time when we don't get fussy about using a pestle and mortar. Use a blender if you like — unless you've become addicted to the mortar by now.

2 handfuls of flat-leaf (Italian) parsley leaves
2 tablespoons Italian pine nuts (not the small Chinese ones)

5 best-quality anchovy fillets in oil
1 garlic clove
20 g (¾ oz) salted capers, rinsed and dried

80 ml (2½ fl oz/⅓ cup) olive oil, plus extra for drizzling
45 ml (1½ fl oz) white wine vinegar
sea salt

If using a blender, place the parsley, pine nuts and anchovies in the blender. Blitz briefly, add the garlic and blitz again. Add the capers, olive oil and vinegar and process until everything is well combined, but with a coarse consistency.

If using a mortar, chop the parsley leaves roughly and set them aside. Pound the pine nuts, anchovies, garlic and capers in the mortar until they are broken up. Add the parsley and keep pounding it against the side of the mortar in a rotary motion. Slowly add the olive oil, drop by drop, mixing all the time. Slowly pour in the vinegar and mix thoroughly.

Scoop the sauce into a bowl, then taste it for salt. Cover with a little more olive oil to stop it discolouring, then set aside until needed. The sauce will keep in the fridge for up to 1 week.

Best with: *Cappon magro* (page 128), roasted or poached meats, and tuna or swordfish steaks.

Caviare d'aubergines *(Eggplant caviar)*

NICE
Serves 4, as a dip
or pasta sauce

The Catalan word *alberginia* and the Provençal word *aubergine* clearly derive from the Arabic word *al-badinjan*, which suggests this Asian fruit may have been introduced to the Mediterranean by the Arabs about 1000 years ago. But the Italians call it *melanzana*, which seems to come from a Greek word meaning 'black', so perhaps we could guess at a Greek role in its spread around the Med, unless it comes from the Latin *mela insana* ('unhealthy apple'). It only appeared in English writings in the 16th century, when it was called 'eggplant' — a name which spread to America and Australia, but disappeared from Britain, where it's called *aubergine* these days. The first recorded reference to it was in a Chinese agricultural text from the year 544 AD.

No matter who brought it, the *alberginia* has been a part of Mediterranean cooking for centuries. In this recipe, we give it a slightly smoky flavour, and blend it with other ancient Med ingredients to make a smooth pulp that feels luxurious. Presumably it is called caviar because of the little black specks visible in it.

*2 large eggplants
(aubergines)*
4 garlic cloves
*sea salt and freshly
ground black
pepper*

*2 fresh oregano sprigs,
leaves picked and
chopped*
2 tablespoons olive oil
*60 g (2¼ oz/½ cup) black
olives, pitted*

*60 g (2¼ oz/⅓ cup) salted
capers, rinsed and
dried*
3 anchovy fillets
5 basil leaves

Preheat the oven to 180°C (350°F). Cut the eggplants in half lengthways. Cut a garlic clove in half and rub it over the cut surface of the eggplants. Make three deep incisions in the flesh, without cutting through to the skin. Season with salt, pepper and the oregano and sprinkle with 1 tablespoon of the olive oil.

Place the eggplant halves, cut side up, in a lightly oiled baking dish. Cover the dish with foil and bake for 1 hour, until the flesh is very tender.

Let the eggplant cool down a little, then scoop out all the flesh, leaving only the skin. Place the flesh in a blender. Peel and crush the three remaining garlic cloves and add to the blender, along with the olives, capers, anchovies, basil and remaining olive oil. Blend for a few seconds, but stop before the mixture becomes too smooth.

You can keep the caviar in a glass jar in the fridge for a week.

Best with: If you are using it on crostini, toast the bread, place some cheese (mozzarella, scamorza, pecorino) on top, bake for a few minutes to let the cheese melt a little, then spread with a generous amount of the caviar and garnish with a few baby basil leaves. It also makes a great dipping sauce for *pinzimonio* (page 56).

If you are using it as a pasta sauce, cook the pasta *al dente*, then drain it, saving a little of the cooking water. Use the water to dilute the caviar and toss it through the pasta (off the heat) with a little olive oil, parmesan cheese and basil leaves.

Beurre Montpellier

Yes, we did say in Chapter 1 that this book is about the way in which olive oil links three regions — and now we're offering you butter. And yes, the elegant town of Montpellier is 20 km (13 miles) inland, so it may not seem a suitable inclusion in a book called *Coastline*. But its speciality is just too good to miss, Montpellier being surrounded by some of France's richest dairy farmland. And this Provençal 'green butter', invented in the 19th century, is usually an accompaniment to cold seafood dishes, which brings us back to the sea.

100 g (3½ oz) mixed fresh leaves, such as watercress, flat-leaf (Italian) parsley, chervil and tarragon
300 g (10½ oz) baby spinach leaves
9 best-quality anchovy fillets in oil, chopped

2 garlic cloves, finely chopped
1 tablespoon salted capers, rinsed and dried
60 g (2¼ oz) cornichons (very small gherkins/ pickles), finely chopped
2 raw egg yolks
3 hard-boiled egg yolks

sea salt and freshly ground black pepper
500 g (1 lb 2 oz) butter, softened but not melted
45–75 ml (1½–2¼ fl oz) olive oil

Have ready a bowl of iced water with some ice. Plunge all the herbs and spinach in boiling water for 30 seconds. Drain and quickly place them in the bowl of iced water to stop the cooking. Drain and squeeze dry with paper towel.

Place the blanched greens in a large mortar with the anchovies, garlic, capers, cornichons, and the raw and hard-boiled egg yolks. Season with a little salt and lots of pepper. Pound into a paste, then add the butter and keep pounding to combine everything thoroughly. Push the mixture through a sieve into a bowl. Add the olive oil and mix with a wooden spoon.

If you are not using a mortar, place the herbs and spinach in a food processor with the anchovies, garlic, capers and cornichons. Season with a little salt and lots of pepper. Process to a smooth paste, then add the raw and cooked egg yolks and the butter. Add the oil and give a final mix.

Roll the mixture into 5 cm (2 inch) long cylinders, wrap in plastic wrap and refrigerate until required. To use, simply cut the butter into discs. If you have any left over, it can be frozen until required.

Best with: The pioneering French chef, Georges Auguste Escoffier, wrote in 1907: 'The only butter fit to be served with cold salmon is Montpellier butter.' It also works with hard-boiled eggs, and cold meats such as veal, beef or pork. And it's a fantastic spread on a sandwich or toast, topped with an anchovy fillet.

Romesco

The citizens of Tarragona are so proud of the Roman origins of their town that they named their favourite sauce after the Italian invaders, even though most of the ingredients would have been unknown to the Romans (tomatoes and red peppers arrived in Europe in the 16th century).

Like all popular dishes, there are many different ways to make romesco — more olive oil, various types of bread, more or less garlic, red or white wine vinegar — but two rules are consistent: the almonds should always be double the quantity of the hazelnuts, and the olive oil should always be double the quantity of the vinegar. We suggest using imported Italian wine vinegars. The Catalans use a dried small pepper called *nyora* (a little similar to what the Americans call *ancho*). It is hard to find outside the region, so we replace these with roasted red capsicums (bell peppers) and hot chilli, with excellent results.

2 large tomatoes, washed and dried	120 g (4¼ oz/¾ cup) blanched almonds	sea salt and freshly ground black pepper
4 whole garlic cloves	60 g (2¼ oz/⅓ cup) peeled hazelnuts	100 ml (3½ fl oz) red wine vinegar
2 red capsicums (bell peppers), quartered and seeded	2 slices of ciabatta 200 ml (7 fl oz) olive oil	1 teaspoon smoked paprika or chilli powder (optional)

Preheat the grill (broiler) to high. Place the whole tomatoes and garlic cloves on a baking tray. Add the capsicum quarters, skin side up, and the place under the grill. Cook for about 15–20 minutes, until the capsicum skins are blackened. Skin the capsicums and the garlic. Peel and seed the tomatoes.

Meanwhile, preheat the oven to 160°C (320°F). Spread the almonds and the hazelnuts on a baking tray and toast in the oven for 8 minutes. Chop the nuts roughly and set aside.

In a frying pan, fry the bread slices on both sides with a little olive oil until golden. Cut off and discard the crusts. Cut the bread into chunks and leave to dry on paper towel.

Pound the roasted garlic in a mortar with a bit of salt, then add the capsicum, tomatoes, the bread and the nuts. Add a little olive oil and pound until you have a smooth paste.

Transfer the mixture to a bowl and stir in more olive oil to make an emulsified sauce. Now add the vinegar and mix thoroughly. If you like a spicy sauce, stir in the paprika or chilli powder.

Let the sauce rest in the fridge for a couple of hours before serving. It will keep in an airtight container for up to 5 days.

Best with:

Romesco was invented to go with seafood (when mint or fennel leaves are sometimes added), but it also works wonderfully with poultry, lamb, beef and vegetables. It's great smothered over grilled prawns (shrimp).

Romesco is also traditionally used with *calçot*, a type of Catalan onion, like a thick shallot, cooked on the barbecue. You're unlikely to find *calçots* outside of Spain, but pencil leeks or fat spring onions (scallions) are a handy substitute. After cooking, they are wrapped in newspaper to keep them warm. When family and friends are ready to eat, they peel off the outer layer and dip them in the sauce. That's a great way to start a meal, with some bruschetta.

BARCELONA (CATALUNYA):
Still serving traditional
favourites from the 19th
century, Can Culleretes
is the oldest restaurant in
Catalunya and the second
oldest restaurant in Spain.

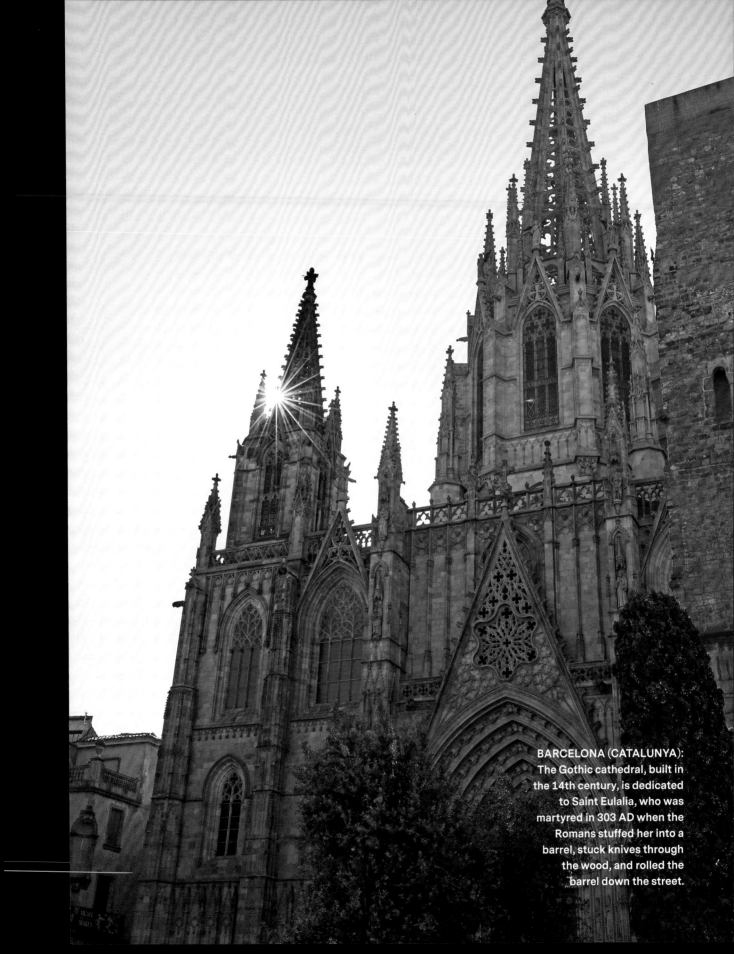

BARCELONA (CATALUNYA):
The Gothic cathedral, built in the 14th century, is dedicated to Saint Eulalia, who was martyred in 303 AD when the Romans stuffed her into a barrel, stuck knives through the wood, and rolled the barrel down the street.

Rouille One

The name of this sauce, really a condiment, means 'rust', because of the colour given to it by the cayenne pepper and the saffron. To the standard mayonnaise ingredients (olive oil, egg yolk, lemon) we can add garlic, chilli and fish stock as a base, then, depending on personal gusto, you might like to add tomato, potatoes, breadcrumbs, roasted capsicums (bell peppers), saffron and even fish livers.

We think some versions are too heavy and complicated for their purpose, which is primarily to complement and enhance fish soups, not to overpower them.

Here are two basic rouilles, one with raw egg yolks and one without.

100 g (3½ oz) baguette, sliced, crusts removed
60 ml (2 fl oz/¼ cup) bouillon (page 196)
3 garlic cloves

sea salt and ground white pepper
2 egg yolks
185 ml (6 fl oz/¾ cup) olive oil

1 teaspoon cayenne pepper
a large pinch of saffron threads
juice of ½ lemon (optional)

Soak the bread in the bouillon for 5 minutes. Squeeze the bread dry, reserving the liquid.

Put the garlic in a mortar with a pinch of salt. Pound with the pestle for 2 minutes, until the garlic is a mushy paste. Add the soaked bread and pound for 2 minutes more, to amalgamate the garlic and the bread.

Transfer the garlic mixture to a bowl. Add the egg yolks and 1 tablespoon of the olive oil. Season with white pepper and mix well with a whisk or wooden spoon.

Add more olive oil slowly, whisking or stirring. When the sauce is firm, stir in the cayenne pepper and the saffron, mixing well. Stir in 1 teaspoon of the reserved bouillon.

Taste for seasoning, and if you prefer a lighter sauce, add the lemon juice.

This rouille will keep in an airtight jar in the fridge for up to 3 days.

Rouille Two

This sauce is much simpler and quicker to make, and we prefer it for bouillabaisse.

100 g (3½ oz) baguette, sliced, crusts removed
60 ml (2 fl oz/¼ cup) bouillon (page 196)

3 garlic cloves
2 red-hot chillies
70 ml (2¼ fl oz) olive oil

a pinch of saffron threads
sea salt and ground white pepper

Soak the bread in the bouillon. Squeeze out the excess liquid, but leave the bread moist.

Place the garlic and chillies in a mortar and pound until you form a paste.

Add the bread and slowly drizzle in the olive oil, stirring constantly, and then the saffron and some salt and white pepper. The sauce should soon reach the consistency of creamy mustard. It will keep in the fridge, covered, for up to 1 week.

Best with: Rouille is traditionally served with fish soups, spread on crostini, which then become boats on top of the soup, or submarines beneath. It can also accompany cold fish or crustacean dishes or enrich salads. Some even dress pasta with it.

Sofregit

Sofregit, like the Italian word *soffritto*, derives from the verb *sofregir* — to fry lightly (or slowly, over low heat). *Sofregit* is considered one of the five fundamental sauces of Catalan cuisine, but like *soffritto*, is not really a sauce on its own, but rather the base for other sauces or soups or stews.

The key ingredients are fresh tomatoes, onions and olive oil. The secret is to perfectly caramelise the onions first and then, slowly and patiently, caramelise the tomatoes.

What follows is the basic, traditional recipe of only onions, tomatoes and olive oil. As for the cooking times, they vary from chef to chef. Some will cook for an hour or more, some think 30 minutes is enough; we're going halfway between them. The essential thing is to cook over low heat so the vegetables retain their flavour.

The Italian *soffritto* has a few more ingredients — sometimes carrots, celery, and herbs such as rosemary, basil and thyme. It's used as the base for sauces, soups and stews, and every chef has his or her own special version.

*60 ml (2 fl oz/¼ cup)
  olive oil
1 onion, thinly sliced*

*a pinch of sea salt
2 garlic cloves,
  chopped*

*200 g (7 oz) ripe red
  tomatoes, peeled, seeded
  and chopped*

Warm the olive oil in a saucepan over medium heat. Add the onion and a pinch of salt and fry, stirring often, for about 15 minutes. Stir in the garlic and cook for 2 minutes more.

Now add the tomatoes, mix thoroughly, turn the heat down to low and simmer for 20 minutes, stirring regularly. Cover and keep to add to sauces such as *Provençal* (page 52).

The sauce will keep in the fridge, covered, for up to 1 week.

SOCCA / FARINATA
Recipe page 189

AÏOLI / ALLIOLI / AGLIATA
Recipe page 53

PROVENÇAL SAUCE
Recipe page 52

PISTOU
Recipe page 36

TAPENADE
Recipe page 65

Provençal *(Tomato and red pepper sauce)*

NICE
Makes about 300 ml
(10½ fl oz)

As with many other recipes in these regions, this sauce has many variations. You will see it done with or without capsicums (bell peppers), with the addition of olives or anchovies or capers, and with all sorts of herbes de Provence. You will even see it with eggplant (aubergine) and zucchini (courgette). This is what we think is the best Provençal sauce, but we have used a Spanish *sofregit* to start it off.

25 g (1 oz) butter
1 tablespoon olive oil
1 red capsicum
   (bell pepper),
   thinly sliced
5 fresh roma (plum)
   tomatoes, peeled,
   seeded and diced

250 ml (9 fl oz/1 cup)
   Sofregit (page 49)
2–3 fresh herb sprigs,
   leaves picked (thyme,
   rosemary and oregano
   are our favourites)
a handful of black olives,
   pitted and sliced

1 teaspoon capers
sea salt and freshly ground
   black pepper

Melt the butter with the oil in a saucepan over medium heat. Fry the capsicum for 5 minutes, then add the tomatoes and fry for another 5 minutes.

Stir in the *sofregit*, herbs, olives and capers and turn the heat down to low. Season with salt and pepper and simmer gently for 20 minutes, stirring regularly.

Use straight away, or keep in an airtight container in the fridge for up to 5 days.

Best with: Try it with fish. Spread the sauce on a plate, top with fried sliced zucchini (courgettes) which you have pan-fried for 3 minutes each side, then pan-fried fillets of whiting or john dory. It also makes a fine pasta sauce. Or it can be a dip sitting next to bowls of *Pistou* (page 36), *Aïoli* (page 53) and *Tapenade* (page 65), waiting for slices of toast or *Socca* (page 189).

Aïoli / Allioli / Agliata

PROVENCE /
CATALUNYA /
LIGURIA
Serves 4, as a dip
or dressing

If you think aïoli is just a mayonnaise into which you dip your chips, take a lesson from Frédéric Mistral, the poet of Provence. He won the Nobel Prize for Literature in 1904, and used the prize money to start a magazine called *L'Aioli*, in honour of his favourite sauce, which, he said, 'saturates the body with warmth and bathes the soul with enthusiasm … Around an aïoli, pungent and yellow-orange as a thread of gold, tell me where you will not find men who recognise each other as brothers. Aïoli epitomises the heat, the power, and the joy of the Provençal sun, but it has another virtue — it drives away flies.'

It's traditionally served on the feast day of the patron saint of any village — with snails at Christmas and with salt cod at Easter.

The Catalans have *allioli* and the Ligurians have *agliata*, but they are pale shadows of the Provençal version, enriched by eggs, lemon and often mustard. Some French recipes suggest two garlic cloves per person if you are making the sauce for an *aïoli monstre*, which involves boiled vegetables and fish covered with creamy waves of the stuff. Our recipe settles for a bit more than one clove per person.

6 garlic cloves
2 pinches of sea salt
1 egg yolk

1 tablespoon lemon juice
185 ml (6 fl oz / ¾ cup)
olive oil

1 teaspoon mild mustard
(optional)

Place the garlic cloves and salt in a mortar and pound until you have a garlic purée or paste. Add the egg yolk and lemon juice and mix with the pestle until all the ingredients are thoroughly combined and have amalgamated.

Now start adding the oil in a thin stream, while constantly mixing using a rotary action. Do not add the oil quickly, or the aïoli will separate. Mix constantly until all the oil is incorporated, and you'll have a wonderful thick, smooth and creamy mayonnaise; stir in the mustard towards the end, if you like it.

(If you don't want to use a mortar, you can achieve a similar effect by using a ceramic or stainless steel bowl, and a whisk. First smash the garlic on a wooden chopping board and, with the flat side of a large knife, work it into a paste. Place the garlic in the bowl with the salt, egg yolk and lemon juice and start whisking. When amalgamated, start adding the oil in a slow stream while whisking continuously.)

Serve immediately, or transfer to a small bowl, cover with plastic wrap and keep in the fridge, where it will last for a couple of weeks.

Variations: The Catalan *allioli* leaves out the eggs and the mustard, and requires at least 20 minutes of pounding to achieve the necessary smoothness. *Agliata*, the Ligurian version, replaces the lemon with white wine vinegar, and the egg yolk with a handful of soft white bread or mashed potato.

Best with: You can turn this into an *aïoli monstre* (aka 'grand aïoli') by pouring the sauce over boiled vegetables (usually carrots, potatoes, artichokes and green beans), and poached white fish (or baccala).

In Catalunya and Liguria, the sauce accompanies grilled or boiled seafood, or is spread on toasted bread, or eaten with green olives or boiled potatoes, the same way sour cream is used. Or try *fegato alla Genovese* — calf liver Genoa-style. Slice the liver thinly. Heat a little olive oil in a non-stick pan and fry the liver to your liking. Put a dollop of *agliata* on the plate and dip each slice of liver into it.

Crema di noci *(Walnut sauce)*

This Ligurian walnut sauce recipe first appeared in the Middle Ages, an evolution of the ancient Roman pesto called *moretum*. The Romans mixed herbs, ricotta cheese, garlic and olive oil into a paste they spread on their bread. We've added the bread into the sauce, along with walnuts and pine nuts, to create a sauce that works on most forms of pasta, but is particularly loved in Liguria when it relaxes over round ravioli called *pansotti* ('little bellies').

250 g (9 oz) shelled walnuts
2 thin slices of ciabatta, crusts removed

60 ml (2 fl oz/¼ cup) milk
2 tablespoons pine nuts
1 garlic clove
75 g (2½ oz/⅓ cup) ricotta cheese

45 ml (1½ fl oz) olive oil
sea salt
1 tablespoon marjoram leaves, finely chopped

Blanch the walnuts in a saucepan of boiling water for 30 seconds, then drain and plunge into iced water to cool. Drain again, place in a tea towel and rub off the papery skins.

Place a few walnuts at a time in a mortar and start pounding.

Soak the bread in the milk for about 5 minutes. Squeeze out the excess liquid, then add the bread to the walnuts. Continue pounding for a minute, then add the pine nuts and garlic. Keep pounding until you achieve a homogenous paste.

Transfer to a bowl, add the ricotta and stir with a wooden spoon to amalgamate. Add the olive oil and a few pinches of salt, then the marjoram, and mix well.

Use straight away, or cover with a thin layer of olive oil and keep in the fridge for up to 1 week.

Best with: Pansotti (ravioli stuffed with spinach) — or mixed, like a picada, into a vegetable soup.

Beurre d'anchois *(Anchovy butter)*

This is a traditional recipe from Liguria, which crept around as far as Nice, to join the Provençal repertoire, so we've given it the Provençal name. Even for a recipe as simple as this, there are so many different versions: with garlic, with capers, with herbs and egg, cold, or made in a pan on medium heat.

20 best-quality anchovy fillets in oil

250 g (9 oz) butter, at room temperature

juice of 1 lemon freshly ground black pepper

Drain the anchovies and chop them into small pieces. Place them in a mortar and pound them to a paste. Add some of the butter and most of the lemon juice and keep pounding.

When the paste is light and soft, place it in a bowl with the rest of the butter and a sprinkling of black pepper. Stir until everything is amalgamated. Taste for seasoning: you might want to add some more black pepper or lemon juice.

Shape the anchovy butter into a thick sausage, wrap it in plastic wrap or waxed paper and refrigerate until needed.

To use, cut the butter into discs. It will keep in the fridge for up to 2 weeks.
Serve with: Spread it on toast, then top with scrambled eggs. Or put a slice on grilled steak or fish. Or use it with spaghetti: while you're boiling the pasta, cut a slice of bread into small cubes and fry them in a tablespoon of anchovy butter. Set them aside, melt another two tablespoons of the butter and toss the (drained) pasta into the frying pan with the butter. Stir the spaghetti, empty it into a bowl, and top it with the croutons.

Acciugata con pinzimonio

(Cold anchovy sauce with raw vegetables)

Pronounced 'achoo-gahta', this is the first of two anchovy sauces designed to be dips for raw or cooked vegetables. This cold one is for summer, to go with what the Ligurians call *pinzimonio* — namely, raw vegetables. The warm one that comes next is for winter, as part of a *bagna cauda*.

15 best-quality anchovy fillets in oil
2 garlic cloves

60 ml (2 fl oz / ¼ cup) olive oil
1 tablespoon white wine vinegar

freshly ground black pepper

In a mortar, pound the anchovies with the garlic. When the paste is smooth, add the olive oil slowly, then the vinegar, and grind on a little black pepper. Mix the sauce thoroughly.

Serve in a bowl, surrounded by crostini, hard-boiled eggs, and sliced tomatoes and seasonal raw vegetables. Your guests can dip into the sauce, or spread it over their chosen ingredients.

The sauce will keep in the fridge for up to 1 week.

Anchoiade / Bagna cauda
(Hot anchovy sauce for dipping vegetables)

Literally, *bagna cauda* means 'warm bath', in which you 'wash' a bunch of vegetables. *Anchoiade* is a sauce from the Piemonte region, which used to be part of Liguria. Seemingly, a salted anchovy merchant from Provence tasted it in Piemonte, liked it and brought it back home, where it was masterfully adapted by the people of Provence, who decided butter would smooth it out. They surrounded it with raw and cooked vegetables for dipping.

Bagna cauda is more than a dish; it's a celebration of conviviality and joy, as you are sharing with friends and family in autumn, particularly during the grape harvest. The bowl of *anchoiade* is kept warm over a candle in a special holder called a *fujot*. It should be accompanied by a glass of rosé.

8 garlic cloves	*300 ml (10½ fl oz)*	*16 best-quality anchovy*
200 g (7 oz) butter	*olive oil*	*fillets*

Slice the garlic very thinly and place in a bowl of cold water. Let it rest for 1 hour.

Drain the garlic slices and dry with paper towels. Place in a flameproof terracotta pan with the butter and half the olive oil. Cook over very low heat for 20 minutes, mixing regularly with a wooden spoon, making sure the garlic doesn't colour. You are aiming to soften and melt the garlic, not fry it.

Use the spoon to mash the garlic into a soft smooth cream. Stir in the anchovies and remaining oil and cook for about 10 minutes, until the anchovies have melted and have created a fragrant light brown cream.

Must be served very hot and immediately. If it's a *bagna cauda*, keep it hot — ideally in a terracotta pan on a rack over a candle!

Best with: Surround it with platters of raw or cooked vegetables — cos lettuce, endive, celery, peeled and seeded cucumber, fennel, radishes, mushrooms, carrots, zucchini (courgettes), cherry tomatoes, capsicums (bell peppers), boiled or raw artichokes (purple is best if raw), baby artichoke hearts, potatoes, asparagus, oven-baked onions, spring onions (scallions) — and grissini (bread sticks).

If they have any *bagna cauda* left, the peasants of Piemonte use it to make scrambled eggs. They also spread it on hard polenta (fried or baked).

PINZIMONIO
Recipe page 56

BAGNA CAUDA
Recipe page 57

Picada

Picada is not so much a sauce as an essential seasoning that is added to a dish towards the end of cooking, to boost flavour, to thicken, to enrich and to unify the ingredients. It apparently originated in the 14th century, when the ingredients considered essential were garlic, parsley, bread, saffron and nuts; later generations added tomatoes, but we prefer the old ways.

The picada, like all the pestos of the Mediterranean, is best prepared in a mortar, at least at the beginning; we don't mind if you finish it off in a blender. The idea is to make a paste so smooth your guests will not notice any nut fragments in their stew — only the luscious depth they contribute to the gravy.

4 garlic cloves, finely chopped
sea salt and freshly ground black pepper
12 blanched almonds, roasted

12 blanched hazelnuts, roasted
1 slice of ciabatta, toasted
a large pinch of saffron threads

2 tablespoons finely chopped flat-leaf (Italian) parsley
3 tablespoons olive oil

In a large mortar, start pounding the garlic with a pinch of salt. When it is well crushed, add the nuts, bread and saffron. Pound them all together until a thick paste is formed. Add the parsley and the olive oil and stir them through.

Best with: Just before serving, stir a dollop of picada into meat stews. It even works with paella. It will keep in the freezer for 6 months.

Xató

Two coastal towns, about halfway between Tarragona and Barcelona, claim to be the source of the sauce that is pronounced like the French word *chateau* — Sitges and Vilanova i la Geltrú. But six other towns, on what is called 'the Xató route', all offer their own recipe for the sauce and the curly endive salad that it usually dresses.

We hope the one we offer here is approximately what is served every January in Vilanova's food carnival, but that doesn't mean we are taking sides.

This one differs from romesco in having no capsicum (bell pepper), no hazelnuts, no tomatoes and no bread, but we've seen *xató* recipes containing all of those ingredients, so feel free to play around to your taste.

4 garlic cloves
12 blanched almonds,
  toasted

sea salt and freshly
  ground black pepper
2 red-hot chillies, halved
  and seeded

125 ml (4 fl oz / ½ cup)
  olive oil
60 ml (2 fl oz / ¼ cup)
  white wine vinegar

In a mortar, place the garlic and the almonds with a pinch of salt. Pound for 2 minutes.

Add the chillies and pound until you have a smooth paste. Gradually blend in the olive oil and vinegar, and taste to see if you need more salt or pepper.

If making this sauce in a blender, put all the ingredients in at once and process until the almonds are reduced to a fine paste.

Use straight away, or keep in the fridge and use within 1 week.

Best with: *Xatonada* salad (page 137), or on a frittata, or as a rub for roast chicken.

LES CALANQUES
(PROVENCE): The 'fjords'
enclosed by limestone cliffs
provide secluded beaches for
swimmers from Marseille.

Saussoun

This is an ancient recipe from Provence, with an unusual combination of flavours and a fantastic freshness and piquancy. Originally it was prepared as a kind of fennel and almond soup, and the farmers' wives would take it into the fields so their husbands could dip their bread in it for mid-morning snacks. It's more often served nowadays as topping on crostini, or generously spread on toasted baguette (rubbed with even more garlic), or as part of an antipasto, or as finger food with cocktails.

1 medium fennel bulb, with fronds
200 g (7 oz/1¼ cups) blanched almonds
60 ml (2 fl oz/¼ cup) olive oil

8 best-quality anchovy fillets, in oil
2 garlic cloves
a large handful of mint leaves

Discard the outer leaves of the fennel. Very finely chop some of the fronds, as well as the fennel bulb.

Place the chopped fennel bits in a food processor. Add the almonds and some of the oil and blend to a rough paste. Now add the anchovies, the garlic and the mint leaves, adding a little more oil. When all is blended into a paste (not too smooth!), transfer the mixture into a bowl and, with a wooden spoon, stir in the rest of the olive oil. You don't have to use all the oil, just as much as you need to make the sauce spreadable.

If you are using a mortar, chop the almonds and set aside. Start pounding the garlic with a bit of salt. Then add the almonds and chopped fennel bits, pounding until a paste is achieved. Add some olive oil and all the other ingredients. If your mortar is not big, mash the ingredients a bit at a time, transferring each batch to a bowl.

The sauce will keep in the fridge, well covered with oil, for about a week.

Best with: When you've spread your *saussoun* onto a bruschetta, sprinkle on some feathery fennel fronds. This also makes a fine pasta sauce — add a little of the cooking water to loosen the paste, and toss a healthy dollop through linguine or fettucine.

Tapenade

This dish gets its name from the Provençal dialect word *tapeno,* which means 'caper', so you'd have to assume these little buds are an essential ingredient. Capers were brought to this part of the Mediterranean by the Greeks around 2500 years ago. They had the habit of keeping the tiny buds preserved in oil in amphoras. The Romans added vinegar and garlic as preservatives, and in the Middle Ages, some genius came up with the notion of including olives.

The three main ingredients — black olives, anchovies and capers — are individually quite strong in flavour, but they magically blend together to form a sauce which is delicate and fragrant. It is usually found on top of tiny toasts, or waiting to receive a scooping slice of *Socca* (a speciality of Nice, see page 189), but in Provence we've had it on seared tuna and swordfish. And it makes a terrific pasta sauce.

The main difference between the Italian version (*paté d'olive*) and the French version is that in Provence, no herbs are used (except basil, occasionally). In Liguria, we like to include rosemary and thyme and a squeeze of lemon. In Catalunya, we've seen thyme, oregano and even cornichons in the mix.

We think the best capers come from the island of Pantelleria (also the sunny source of one of Italy's greatest dessert wines, Passito di Pantelleria), but we're happy with any small capers (preserved in salt, which is washed off for this recipe). The best olives are the tiny black ones called *taggiasca,* which grow near Genoa and near Nice under the name *cailletier.*

We suggest making this with a pestle and mortar, but a blender will still give a good result (not too smooth, please).

1 sprig each of thyme, *oregano and rosemary,* *leaves picked*	*500 g (1 lb 2 oz)* *taggiasca black olives* *2 garlic cloves* *6 brown anchovy fillets* *(see page 19)*	*a generous tablespoon* *of salted capers, rinsed* *and dried* *125 ml (4 fl oz / ½ cup)* *olive oil*

Pick the leaves from the herb sprigs and roughly chop them. Crush the olives with the flat of the knife and remove the seeds.

Pound the garlic cloves in a mortar for 2 minutes, then add the herbs and pound for another minute. Add the olives and capers and keep pounding until everything is amalgamated. Add the anchovies and pound until you have a coarse paste in which pieces of olives are still visible.

Add the olive oil and stir it through, and your tapenade is ready. It is best used straight away, but will keep in an airtight container in the fridge for up to 5 days.

Best with: Put this on crostini and grilled fish, or use it as a sauce with a hard pasta such as spaghetti.

Chapter Three

ANTIPASTO / HORS D'OEUVRES / TAPES

Snacks & Starters

CASSIS (PROVENCE):
A warm evening must
begin with *l'heure de l'apero*
— a ritual involving sips and
snacks, which the Spanish
and Italians call *aperitivo*.

Small is beautiful

Europe has generated many different names for the little treats that precede a meal or join a drink, but the word that has conquered the world is tapas.

Literally meaning 'lids', the word *tapas* apparently refers to the saucers that were placed on top of wine glasses to keep the flies out (or your friends from sipping your drink).

We were going to call this chapter 'Tapas' until we discovered that word originated with the Castillian Spaniards, not the Catalans (who would be more at home with 'Aperitius', but would grudgingly allow 'Tapes'). The Italian term 'antipasto' (literally 'before the meal', *not* 'before the pasta') and the French term 'hors d'oeuvre' (literally 'outside the major work') are still serviceable, even if they sound a bit old-fashioned in societies that prefer to graze rather than dine. More modern are *amuse-bouches* ('entertain mouths') from France; *assaggi* (tastings) or *sfizi* (whims) or *passatempi* (pastimes) from Italy; and *cazuelas* (small pots) or *cojonuda* (hot chick) or *cojonudo* (hot guy) from Spain.

We might even have got away with calling the chapter 'Mezze', since we're attributing much of the shared culture of the Med to the Greeks.

For a while we were also keen on 'Stuzzichini', a Ligurian term that comes from *stuzzichare*, to poke or provoke (so they could be seen as 'palate teasers'). The problem is that English speakers would have trouble pronouncing it, softening the 'ch' as they often do with bruschetta, even though Italians always pronounce 'ch' like a *k*, as in chianti and zucchini.

The essence of all these terms is 'something to nibble with a drink'. All over Spain (and in much of Italy) there is the culture of the *aperitivo*: having a couple of glasses and a few snacks at the bar before sitting down for lunch or dinner. The Catalans call the ritual doing a *vermut*, in honour of the drink vermouth, a fortified wine flavoured with herbs, traditionally consumed during *aperitivo*. In Italy nowadays, *aperitivo* is often called *l'appy hour*, and the drink is more likely to be prosecco or Campari than vermouth.

In Catalunya, the pre-lunch *vermut* is accompanied by very light snacks. The pre-dinner snacks are more substantial, because the Catalans dine late — 9 pm at the earliest — and need sustenance earlier in the evening. But these snacks never achieve the size of tapas.

All of these tiny treats are consumed when you're out. Choosing and adapting them for this chapter, we were thinking about dishes that you'd want to make at home, perhaps when friends are coming over to join the family for a long afternoon of sipping and chewing and chatting. So here you'll find some classic *pintxos*, *amuse-bouches*, *stuzzichini* and *mezze* that are easy to prepare and easy to share with a bunch of noisy drinkers.

Ideally, there'll be enough left over for you to snack on the next day.

Pa amb tomaquet *(Tomato bread)*

BARCELONA
Serves 6, as part
of a tapas spread

The Catalans are so fond of this form of crostini they eat it for breakfast, and give it to their children every afternoon when they return from school. It depends on having a very ripe tomato, so it's best consumed in late summer. The olive oil should be the best extra virgin you can find. The bread should be good quality rustic style. The garlic is optional — Catalan purists would not use it, but we think it transforms this toast from a breakfast staple to a pre-dinner delight.

3 garlic cloves
12 slices ciabatta

6 very ripe tomatoes
olive oil

sea salt

Preheat oven to 180°C (350°F). Cut the garlic cloves in half. Lightly toast the bread in the oven for 5 minutes and enthusiastically rub each slice with the cut sides of the garlic.

Cut each tomato in half and rub a half tomato onto each piece of toast, trying to force all the juicy red pulp into the bread, but leaving the skin in your hand (to throw away). Sprinkle with olive oil and salt and eat quickly, before the bread goes soggy.

If the tomatoes are not soft and luscious, grate them into a bowl and stir in 2 tablespoons olive oil. If you're a garlic addict, you can make a paste in a mortar with garlic, salt and a little olive oil, and spread it on the bread before spooning on the grated tomatoes.

Best with: Catalans say *Pa amb tomaquet* is a meal in itself, but they're not averse to topping it with an anchovy, a slice of ham (called *jamón* in Spain, *pernil* in Catalunya or *prosciutto* in Italy), or a slice of manchego cheese or sprinkling of grated pecorino.

NICE (PROVENCE):
The street signs are
in French and in Nissa
dialect, which has more
in common with Ligurian.

RUE
DU JÉSUS
CARRIERA
DÓU JÈSU

RUE
BENOÎT BUNICO
CARRIERA
DE L'ARC

LE BISTRO DU FROM

Restaurant de F

Petits farcis *(Stuffed vegetables)*

The Nice name for this dish translates literally as 'little stuffed'. In Liguria it's known more prosaically as *verdure ripiene* (stuffed vegetables). Essentially it involves hollowing out vegetables, spicing and frying what you took out of them, putting the filling back in and baking them. How the stuffing is spiced varies from village to village, and in wealthier areas can include a little beef or lamb, but ours is a vegetarian version.

4 zucchini (courgettes)
2 capsicums (bell peppers)
8 small eggplants (aubergines)
4 white onions
2 slices ciabatta, crusts removed
80 ml (2½ fl oz/⅓ cup) milk

2 eggs
200 ml (7 fl oz) olive oil
a pinch of freshly grated nutmeg
2 garlic cloves, finely chopped
2 oregano sprigs, leaves picked and chopped

1 marjoram sprig, leaves picked and chopped
100 g (3½ oz) freshly grated parmesan
sea salt and freshly ground black pepper
60 g (2¼ oz/½ cup) dry breadcrumbs

Trim the ends off the zucchini and slice them in half, lengthways. Core the capsicums, cut them in halves and remove any remaining seeds from the inside. Cut the tops off the eggplants, then halve them lengthways. Peel the onions and cut them in half.

Soften the vegetables for 5 minutes in a saucepan of boiling water. Meanwhile, soak the bread in the milk for 5 minutes. Drain the vegetables and pat dry.

Preheat the oven to 180°C (350°F).

Using a spoon, scoop out the middles of the zucchini, eggplants and onions, leaving a thick shell. Place all the vegetable pulps in a mixing bowl and mash them. Add the soaked bread to the mash. Add the eggs, most of the olive oil, the nutmeg, all the garlic, and half the oregano, marjoram and parmesan. Season with salt and pepper and mix together thoroughly.

Lightly oil a baking oven tray, then place the vegetable shells on it. Fill each shell with stuffing, not too tightly packed. Sprinkle the breadcrumbs on top of each shell, drizzle with the remaining oil and bake in the oven for 25 minutes.

Sprinkle on the remaining oregano, marjoram and parmesan and serve.

Ratatouille / Samfaina

(Spicy vegetable stew)

The French word *ratatouille* and the Italian word *ratatuia* are variants of the French word *touiller,* which means 'to stir'. The Catalan word *samfaina* is far more poetic, meaning 'symphony'.

Although Nice is legendary for its ratatouille, the Catalans are probably right in claiming they were the first to make this dish, because they were the first people in Europe to embrace the peppers and tomatoes that came from America in the early 1500s (their word *tomaquet* is from the Aztec *tomatl,* while the Italians invented their own word for the exotic new fruit — *pomodoro,* which means 'golden apple').

A *samfaina* is cooked a little longer than a ratatouille, because the Catalans think of it as a sauce, to be stirred into other dishes, while the Niçois think of it as a dish in itself. The Ligurians make a whole vegetarian meal of it, adding green beans and borlotti beans to what is already a complex of textures and flavours.

Our version gives you the option of going light or going substantial, but either way, make plenty of garlic-rubbed toast for your guests to dip into it. Or serve it as a side dish with grilled pork ribs, rabbit, chicken, tuna or swordfish steaks. It can also be a topping for the Catalan pizza known as *Coca* (page 182).

100 ml (3½ fl oz) olive oil
2 garlic cloves, chopped
2 eggplants (aubergines),
 peeled and diced
2 red capsicums (bell
 peppers), sliced into strips
1 yellow capsicum (bell
 pepper), sliced into strips
3 medium zucchini
 (courgettes)

300 g (10½ oz) ripe
 tomatoes, peeled, seeded
 and chopped
250 ml (9 fl oz/1 cup)
 Sofregit (page 49)
3 thyme sprigs, leaves
 picked and chopped
3 basil sprigs, leaves picked
 and chopped
1 teaspoon smoked paprika

Optional
400 g (14 oz) fresh borlotti
 beans, shelled
300 g (10½ oz) green beans,
 trimmed and chopped
 into 2–3 pieces each

If you want to make a Ligurian ratatuia, cook the borlotti beans in salted boiling water for about 30 minutes, and boil the green beans for 2 minutes; drain and set aside. Add them when you're adding the herbs, towards the end of the cooking process.

To make the ratatouille or samfaina, heat the olive oil in a large saucepan over medium heat and add the garlic, eggplant, capsicums and zucchini. Cook for 6 minutes, stirring often. Add the tomatoes, then cover and cook for another 4 minutes.

Stir in the *sofregit* and simmer, uncovered, for about 15 minutes, until the vegetables are soft — or longer if you want them mushy.

Now stir in the thyme, basil and paprika and cook for another 2 minutes.

You can keep the ratatouille/samfaina in a sealed jar in the fridge for up to a week.

RIOMAGGIORE (LIGURIA): The southernmost of the five fishing villages in the Cinque Terre, first settled in the 13th century, marks the beginning of the walking trail called the Via dell'Amore.

Patates braves

(Fried potatoes with allioli and romesco)

BARCELONA
Serves 4, as part
of a tapas spread

This is one of the greatest potato dishes in the world, which is surprising because the potato arrived in Spain less than 500 years ago (from Peru, where it was first cultivated by the Inca people 7000 years ago). Garlic, the other main ingredient of this dish, had been in the Mediterranean much longer, and was clearly just waiting for the perfect vegetable accompaniment.

Patates braves (which the Castillians call *patatas bravas*) are usually enjoyed as tapas, but they are also a fine side dish with grilled meats.

For best results, the cubes of potato must be really crisp. To achieve that, it's vital to let the boiled potatoes cool and air-dry in a colander — or even better, on a wire rack — before frying them.

They can be served with just paprika and garlic mayonnaise, but there are many variations. We offer the version most loved along the Mediterranean coast.

½ teaspoon sea salt
2 bay leaves
a pinch of ground cumin
4 large starchy potatoes
   (sebago are ideal)

sunflower, cottonseed
   or vegetable oil, for
   shallow-frying to
   a depth of at least
   4 cm (1½ inches)
Allioli (page 53), to serve
Romesco (page 44),
   to serve

Savoury salt
1 teaspoon sea salt
1 teaspoon freshly ground
   black pepper
2 pinches of smoked
   paprika
a pinch of cayenne
   pepper (optional)

Bring 1 litre (35 fl oz/4 cups) water to the boil. Add the salt, bay leaves and cumin, then reduce the heat to a simmer.

Peel the potatoes and cut them into 2 cm (1 inch) cubes, keeping them in cold water until you are ready to use them.

Add the potato cubes to the simmering water, bring back to the boil, then cook them for 10 minutes. They should be tender but still firm. Strain the potatoes, then leave them on a wire rack to cool and dry for at least 20 minutes.

Combine the savoury salt ingredients, adding a pinch of cayenne pepper if you'd like it spicy.

Pour the oil into a high-sided saucepan, to a depth of about 4 cm (1½ inches). Put the pan over low heat and after 5 minutes, add the potatoes.

Fry for about 5 minutes, turning the potatoes with a slotted spoon, until they're turning amber. Turn the heat up to high and cook for another 6 minutes, until golden brown and crunchy.

Strain them out of the oil, placing them on paper towel to soak off some of the oil.

Transfer the potatoes to a bowl and toss them with the savoury salt. Serve quickly.

If you're serving them as tapas, present them with small bowls of allioli and romesco, and plenty of toothpicks so people can stab and dip. If they're a side dish with meat, pour the allioli and romesco over them in the bowl, creating a beautiful pattern of white and pink.

Truita de patates *(Potato tortilla)*

Here's another regional debate in which we're carefully not taking sides: is the Catalan *tortilla* a simplified version of a *frittata*, or is the Ligurian *frittata* just an over-complicated *tortilla*? Both are a kind of omelette, sliced and served as part of an array of snacks. We note these differences: tortilla is always made with potatoes, and is flipped in the frying pan and finished on the top of the stove. Frittata doesn't necessarily contain potato, and may be finished in the oven.

The Castillian word *tortilla* (Catalan *truita*) means a round cake, and when the Spanish arrived in the Americas in the 16th century, they used it to describe the pancakes cooked by the Aztecs (hence its modern usage in Mexican restaurants). That suggests the Spaniards were already making tortillas, but before the 16th century these could not have contained potatoes, which were brought to Europe in the 1530s. The Basque people of Bilbao, just north of Spain, claim the potato version was invented there in the 1830s, and then spread south. We're giving it to Girona, which is as close to Bilbao as our travels took us.

3 medium potatoes, peeled	*420 ml (14½ fl oz/1⅔ cups) olive oil*	*5 eggs* *sea salt*
	1 large white onion	

Quarter the potatoes lengthways, then slice them thinly crossways.

In a large non-stick frying pan, warm the olive oil over medium heat. When it's hot, add the potato and cook for about 6 minutes, turning regularly. The slices should cook but not brown.

Chop the onion finely and add it to the potato. Mix and cook for another 15 minutes. Strain the mixture using a colander, reserving the cooking oil, and allow the potato and onion to cool.

Break the eggs into a large bowl, season with salt and whisk. Add the onion and potato mix to the eggs and stir thoroughly.

Pour the reserved cooking oil back into the pan and place it over high heat for 2 minutes. Pour the potato and egg mixture into the oil and shake the pan to spread it evenly. Cook for 4 minutes, then turn the omelette over and cook for another 4 minutes.

(Alternatively, you could cook the omelette in an ovenproof frying pan, by putting the pan in a preheated 180°C/350°F oven for 15 minutes, or under a hot grill/broiler for 5 minutes.)

Slide the tortilla onto a plate. Let it set for 5 minutes, then slice into wedges and serve.

A cavalcade of crostini

In Liguria, a small piece of toast with a tasty topping is called a *crostino* (plural: *crostini*). A *bruschetta* is the same thing, except that it usually has garlic rubbed on the toast (and, English-speaking waiters please note, it's pronounced broo-sketta).

The French equivalent is *canapé*, which literally means 'a sofa' (upon which the topping reclines, presumably). The Catalan equivalent is a *montadito*, which literally means 'little mounted'.

Here are some suggestions for toppings that can be mounted upon crunchy couches in your kitchen.

The bread we suggest you use is the large baguette sometimes called 'Italian bread' or *pane di casa*, which gives oval-shaped slices (not more than a centimetre, or half an inch, thick). You should toast the slices briefly, or fry them on both sides in a very hot metal pan with a tiny amount of oil. The point is to create a hard surface for the topping to sit on and a crunchy texture when you bite, but no burnt bits to spoil the flavour.

All the thicker sauces and pastes in the previous chapter can be joyfully spread on crostini; our favourites are *Tapenade* (page 65), *Salsa verde* (page 41) and *Romesco* (page 44). Most of the *pintxos* on pages 90–91 sit comfortably on lightly toasted bread. Or you can finely chop the mussels *in escabeche* (page 91) and spread that mixture on toast with some chopped rocket (arugula). Now let's get a little more ambitious.

Salsa marò

In the spring, fresh broad beans can be double-peeled and mashed in a mortar with olive oil, chopped garlic and mint leaves, then stirred with grated pecorino cheese before spreading on toast. This was a 10th-century Arab contribution to Ligurian cuisine (the name comes from the Arab word *mara*, which means a condiment).

Eggplant

Cut an eggplant (aubergine) into slices about 1 cm (½ inch) thick. Finely chop a garlic clove and marinate it in olive oil with thyme leaves. Paint the mixture onto the eggplant slices and grill (broil) until they start to brown (about 6 minutes). Place each grilled eggplant slice on a slice of toasted bread. Top with a slice of manchego cheese or goat's cheese, put back under the grill (broiler) for 2 minutes, sprinkle with olive oil and serve.

Brandade (a Provençal classic)

Soak baccala (dried salt cod) in fresh water for 48 hours, changing the water four times to remove most of the salt. Boil the baccala with a bay leaf for 10 minutes. When it has cooled, remove all the skin and bones, break the cod into small pieces and stir it through mashed potato which has been made with full-cream milk. Cook a finely chopped garlic clove in about 100 ml (3½ fl oz) olive oil for 2 minutes, then stir that through the mashed potato. Dollop a tablespoon on each piece of toast, then sprinkle with finely chopped parsley and a grind of black pepper.

Tuna tartare

Finely chop a handful of oregano and thyme leaves, 2 teaspoons capers (rinsed to remove excess salt), a handful of pitted black olives and ½ red onion. Add the juice of ½ lemon and a big splash of olive oil and stir thoroughly. Just before serving, finely cube a piece of tuna and stir that through the olive and caper mixture. Spoon it onto toasts.

Prawns and scallops

Sear peeled small raw prawns (shrimp) and scallops for 1 minute on each side. Place 1 prawn and 1 scallop on top of each slice of toasted bread (or place them back in the scallop shells). Brush the seafood with a vinaigrette of olive oil, lemon juice and chopped fresh red chilli.

Chicken livers

Trim and chop 200 g (7 oz) chicken livers and fry them for 5 minutes in olive oil with 3 chopped sage leaves. Finely chop 5 anchovies, 1 teaspoon pine nuts, 1 teaspoon rinsed capers, 3 pitted black olives and the leaves from 1 oregano sprig. Add them to the livers with a tablespoon of butter. Stir through to warm over medium heat for 1 minute. Spoon onto toast and serve immediately.

CROSTINI WITH:
EGGPLANT *(recipe page 82)*,
SALSA MARÒ *(page 82)*,
TUNA TARTARE *(page 83)*,
CHICKEN LIVERS *(page 83)*.

Ligurians use the word 'crostino' for a little snack on a toasted slice of baguette, and 'bruschetta' when the toasted bread has been rubbed with oil and garlic.

SCALLOPS WITH PRAWNS
Recipe page 83

Frittata ai peperoni

(Omelette with peppers)

Serves 4

The word *frittata* derives from a word for 'fried', and was the Italian word for a simple omelette until a more elaborate (tall, plump) version was popularised in the mid 20th century. Wedges of frittata are now essential in any antipasto spread. The fillings vary seasonally; we think red capsicums are stimulating for both the eyes and the tongue.

4 red capsicums (bell peppers)
2 tablespoons olive oil

2 garlic cloves, finely chopped
5 eggs
a pinch of sea salt

4 mint sprigs, leaves picked and chopped
50 g (1¾ oz / ½ cup) grated parmesan cheese

Burn the capsicums until blistered (see page 21), then remove the skin, stalks and seeds. Finely slice the flesh.

Splash some of the olive oil into a wide ovenproof frying pan and fry the garlic for 2 minutes over medium heat. Add the sliced capsicum and fry for 2 minutes. Scoop the mixture out of the pan and set it aside in a bowl, leaving the pan coated with oil.

Preheat the oven to 180°C (350°F), or a grill (broiler) to medium–high. Break the eggs into a bowl. Season with a pinch of salt, add the mint and parmesan and whisk until everything is amalgamated. Stir in the capsicum and garlic mixture.

Splash a little more oil into the frying pan in which the capsicum strips were cooked, then place over medium heat for 2 minutes. Pour in the egg mixture, shaking the pan to spread it evenly (or use a spatula). Cover and cook for 5 minutes, or until the bottom is set.

Place the pan in the preheated oven for 15 minutes, or under a hot grill (broiler) for about 5 minutes to set the top half.

Slide the frittata onto a plate, then let it rest for at least 5 minutes. Slice the frittata into wedges and serve.

MARSEILLE (PROVENCE):
Around 2600 years ago, the
Greeks gave the name 'Massalia'
to the first trading post they set
up in France, living harmoniously
at first with the local Liguri tribe.

A parade of pintxos

Tapas is not a Catalan word, although tourist restaurants in Barcelona are happy to use it, as are cafés across the border in France, where the laneways of Collioure are lined with blackboards offering French dishes called *Nos tapas du moment* ('Our snacks of the moment').

For the Catalans, tapas are not small enough to be bar snacks, and not big enough to be part of a proper meal. They prefer to use the Basque word *pintxos* (pronounced 'pinchos') for their drinking nibbles. It means 'spikes' — a reference to the thick toothpicks or thin skewers that hold the ingredients together and allow you to pick them up from the saucers that line the bar.

El Xampanyet restaurant in Barcelona displays this chalkboard sign for the benefit of English-speaking visitors:

HOW TO EAT PINTXOS. STEP BY STEP.
1. We give you a plate.
2. Take by yourself the 'cold' pintxos that you like.
3. Order the 'hot' pintxos to the maîtres.
4. Keep all the sticks on your plate. We count later. DON'T EAT ANY STICK!

Here are a few examples of pintxos you might prepare as party food. Not all of our suggestions originated in Catalan country, but we think Catalans would enjoy them.

Olives

Olives are ideal for spiking. Wrap a white anchovy around and through a large green pitted olive, keeping it together with a toothpick.

Mix together a handful of black olives (Niçoise or Taggiasca, if you can get them), a handful of green olives (ideally Sicilian), and a handful of purple olives (Kalamata) — all pitted. Splash on a generous amount of olive oil, and stir it through the olives with the leaves from 1 rosemary sprig and 1 thyme sprig, the zest of ½ lemon, and a generous pinch of chilli flakes. Toss them in a frying pan over low heat for 5 minutes, then leave the mixture to marinate for a day. Warm them again before serving.

Ham or prawns or figs

Set a square of jamón (or prosciutto) on a square of manchego (or pecorino) cheese, splash with the best olive oil and spike. Instead of jamón you could use hot salami, which you've sliced and grilled for 5 minutes.

Slice 4 zucchini (courgettes) into thin discs. Grill (broil) the discs with a little olive oil for 5 minutes. Spread a little cream cheese on each disc. Grill 10 peeled prawns (shrimp), chop them into quarters and put 1 piece of prawn between 2 slices of zucchini, holding them together with toothpicks.

Cut figs in half and marinate them for a few minutes in olive oil, finely chopped garlic and some good balsamic vinegar. Place a slice of goat's cheese on each fig half and bake them in the oven at 180°C (350°F) for 5 minutes. Pin them together with toothpicks when you take them out of the oven.

All of the above can be served on pieces of toasted bread, which you could then call *crostini* (or *bruschetta* if you rub garlic on the bread). See pages 82–83 for more on that.

Peppers or sausages

Burn and skin (see page 21) 1 red, 1 green and 1 yellow capsicum (bell pepper) and cut them into strips. Intersperse the colours on a long platter. Lay an anchovy fillet along each strip, sprinkle with a little rosemary and splash with the best olive oil. Stab.

Grill 5 fennel sausages and 5 long green chillies. Slice the sausages, slice the chillies, and put a slice of chilli on each bit of sausage. A toothpick keeps them together.

A myriad of mussels

Mussels look lovely served in their bottom shells. To prepare them, cook them in a covered pan over high heat for 5 minutes, and take them out when they have opened. Rip off the top shells, squeeze on a little lemon juice, and you have your first mussel pintxo. Keep the water they release as a seafood stock.

Or you can be more ambitious. Fry chopped garlic and parsley together in olive oil for 2 minutes with a little freshly ground black pepper, mix it with a little of the liquid the mussels have released, and spoon that onto them.

For *muscoli gratinati* (*moules au gratin*), top the opened mussels with a mix of butter, chopped garlic and herbs (tarragon and thyme for Provençal; parsley and oregano for Ligurian). Sprinkle with dry breadcrumbs and bake in a 180ºC (350ºF) oven for 5 minutes, until the butter melts and browns the crumbs. For the baking, it's helpful to sit the mussel shells in a bed of rock salt so they don't tip over and spill the precious herb butter.

For mussels Catalan style, make a *Sofregit* (page 49) and stir in 1 tablespoon smoked paprika. Spoon that over the opened mussels in their shells.

Or make mussels *in escabeche* (Catalan *escabetx*, Ligurian *scabeccio*), which essentially means pickling them. Heat them until they open, remove from their shells and toss in plain (all-purpose) flour. Fry in hot olive oil for 1 minute each side, then marinate for at least 2 hours in a mix of 1 tablespoon white wine vinegar, 4 tablespoons olive oil, 1 crushed garlic clove and the leaves from 1 rosemary sprig. Serve in their half-shells, or spread them on a platter for your guests to stab with their toothpicks.

Or you can force open raw mussels and stuff them with a mixture of finely chopped prawn (shrimp) meat, garlic, oregano, parmesan cheese and a beaten egg; allow 1 peeled prawn and 1 teaspoon of beaten egg for every 4 mussels you plan to stuff. Press the mussel shells closed again and simmer them for 20 minutes in a pot full of *Sofregit* (page 49). Serve them in a big bowl with plenty of bread for dipping into the sauce. Probably forks would make life easier than toothpicks in this case.

Stuffed calamari

The pinnacle of pintxos! Clean 5 small calamari, discarding the innards but keeping the tentacles. Fill the 5 white calamari sacs with this mixture: finely chopped tentacles, onion and garlic, fried together for 10 minutes, then mashed with grated parmesan, parsley and a slice of bread that has been soaked in milk (seasoned with salt and pepper). Seal the calamari parcels with toothpicks, brown for 2 minutes on each side, then simmer them for 25 minutes in *Sofregit* (page 49). Cut the stuffed calamari into slices 1 cm (½ inch) thick. Serve, splashed with a little cooking liquid, on a platter with some strong toothpicks, so guests can spike them and pop them into their mouths.

PEPPERS WITH ANCHOVIES
Recipe page 91

STUFFED MUSSELS
Recipe page 91

FENNEL SAUSAGES WITH GREEN CHILLI
Recipe page 91

**CROSTINI WITH FIG
& GOAT'S CHEESE**
Recipe page 90

**CROSTINI WITH PROSCIUTTO
& MANCHEGO**
Recipe page 90

MARINATED OLIVES
Recipe page 90

Xampinyons i gambes

(Mushroom and prawn bites)

Some purist French chefs declare that you should only put ingredients together in a dish if they would be found together in nature. The cooks in north-east Catalunya would laugh at this notion, pointing out that the idea of combining the bounty of the ocean with the bounty of the soil goes back at least to the ancient Romans. They have a specialty called *Mar i muntanya* ('Sea and mountain'), which we explain in its full splendour in Chapter 8 (page 222). Here is a miniature version of *Mar i muntanya*, ideal as part of a tapas banquet.

5 garlic cloves
sea salt and freshly
  ground black pepper
100 ml (3½ fl oz) olive
  oil

chilli flakes, to taste
12 medium raw prawns
  (shrimp)
12 champignons, stalks
  removed

2 tablespoons finely
  chopped flat-leaf
  (Italian) parsley

Place the garlic cloves and a pinch of salt in a mortar and pound until the garlic is creamy. Pour in about 3 tablespoons of the olive oil and some chilli flakes and mix thoroughly. Pour the garlic chilli oil into a bowl.

Peel and devein the prawns, discarding the shells, but keeping the heads on. Marinate the prawns in the garlic chilli oil for 30 minutes.

Warm a non-stick frying pan over medium heat, then splash in the remaining olive oil. When hot, add the mushrooms to the pan, stalk side up, and brush with the garlic chilli oil. Cook gently for 3 minutes, then turn them over. Cook for a further 2 minutes, then sprinkle with the parsley. Remove the mushrooms from the pan and arrange on a serving plate.

Pour the garlic-marinated prawns into the same pan. Add a sprinkling of chilli flakes and fry the prawns for 2 minutes on each side.

Arrange the prawns on top of the mushrooms and serve.

Llagostins embolicats en les ametlles

(Prawns in almond batter)

Yes, alright, a prawn would not eat an almond in nature (nor vice versa, presumably), but that does not disqualify this dish from consideration in fine dining, or even simple snacking. This is another example of the north-eastern Catalan craze for *Mar i muntanya* ('Sea and mountain'; page 222), combining the best of two worlds in a way that seems peculiar to the neighbours in Provence, and a delightful contrast of textures and tastes to the Catalans.

65 g (2½ oz/½ cup) plain (all-purpose) flour
sea salt

250 g (9 oz/2 cups) sliced almonds
50 g (1¾ oz/½ cup) dry breadcrumbs

16 raw prawns (shrimp), peeled and deveined, tails left on
vegetable oil, for deep-frying

Put the flour in a bowl with a pinch of salt. Whisk in enough water — about 250 ml (9 fl oz/1 cup) — to make a thin batter, whisking until smooth. (For extra flavour, you can squeeze the liquid from the prawn heads into the batter.)

Mix the almonds and breadcrumbs in a bowl. Holding the prawns by the tail, dip them into the batter and allow the excess to drain off, then coat them with the almond mix, pressing it on with your fingers to coat properly.

Heat about 3 cm (1½ inches) of vegetable oil in a saucepan. When it is hot, fry the prawns for 2 minutes each side, or until the coating is golden brown, turning them once.

Drain briefly on paper towel and serve.

Gambes al pil-pil *(Garlic prawns)*

Supposedly the idea of sizzling prawns with garlic and chilli in a terracotta bowl originated in Andalucia, at the opposite end of Spain from Catalunya, but the dish has now been so thoroughly embraced by the bodegas of Barcelona that we just had to include it. In Italy, wiping up sauce (or spicy oil) from the bottom of your bowl is called doing a *scarpetta* — literally 'little shoe', because of the scoop shape into which you form your slice of bread.

250 ml (9 fl oz/1 cup) olive oil
4 dried hot chillies, sliced thinly, seeds removed

3 garlic cloves, thinly sliced
1 kg (2 lb 4 oz) small raw prawns (shrimp), peeled and deveined

crusty bread, to serve
basil, to garnish (optional)

Pour the olive oil into a large frying pan. Add the chilli and garlic. Place over medium heat and gently sizzle the mixture for 2 minutes. Add the prawns, raise the heat and fry for 2 minutes, stirring regularly. Pour the mixture, with the oil, into terracotta bowls (one for each guest). Serve immediately, while still sizzling, with lots of crusty bread for dipping into the oil. To make this more Ligurian, sprinkle on a little chopped basil.

**MUSHROOM &
PRAWN BITES**
Recipe page 94

**PRAWNS IN
ALMOND BATTER**
Recipe page 95

BARCELONA (CATALUNYA):
In the Sant Josep market, the
Santiago family run a dining
counter that pulsates from
breakfast to *aperitivo*.

The Med's mightiest mercat

Breakfast time in Barcelona, and families are queuing to sit on the stools along the counter of Quiosc Modern, in the middle of the Mercat de Sant Josep de la Boqueria, the biggest of the city's ten food markets. The people lucky enough to grab a stool are tucking in to squid and eggs, grilled clams, *Esqueixada de bacallá* (salt cod salad; page 137), tripe with chickpeas and chorizo, grilled octopus, fried artichokes and seared green chillies called pebrots (described by one customer as 'very sweet; only one in 100 is hot' — so it's a kind of Catalan roulette).

At any other time of day, what we're eating would be called tapas, but the Santiago family is too busy to discuss breakfast labelling. They are typical stallholders in the most exhilarating food market in Europe: La Boqueria di Sant Josep. They've been here since the early 2000s. The market has been here since 1217, its name apparently coming from *boc*, a dialect word for 'goat', which must have been sold here back then. Barcelona has been here since 600 BC, when it was settled by Phocaean Greeks (from what is now western Turkey), who let the Romans name it Barcino in 100 BC.

It would be easy to sit on a stool at Quiosc Modern nibbling snacks and reflecting on history all day, making occasional forays into the market to check out the seasonal flow of vegetables and meat and seafood (assuming you could persuade someone to guard your stool). But when Quiosc Modern closes at 7 pm, you'll need to start thinking of your dinner venue.

For scholars of Catalan *cuina* (cooking), that would have to be Can Culleretes: the oldest restaurant in Barcelona, and the second oldest restaurant in Spain. Under vast paintings of fruit, veg and aristocratic excesses, they've been serving pretty much the same menu since 1786. It offers an opportunity to see what real Catalan food is, or was, all about, in a city which has become expert at offering what Americans and Germans imagine is Spanish food.

Visual presentation is not the primary concern of the Agut-Manubens family, who run Can Culleretes. It's getting big servings of tasty food onto the table fast — and if any dish is not tasty enough for you, the bowls of allioli and romesco will help you give it a boost. Some menu examples (written in Spanish, not Catalan, because when this restaurant started, Barcelona was firmly under the control of the Castillian king in Madrid) are: *Butifarra con judias* (pork sausage and white beans); *Pato con ciruelas* (Duck with prunes); *Espinacas a la Catalana* (spinach with raisins and pine nuts); and *Pollo con samfaina* (chicken with ratatouille).

You'll find some of the dishes from Quiosc Modern and Can Culleretes in this book. We hope we haven't modernised them too much.

BARCELONA (CATALUNYA):
The boqueria market, which
opened in the year 1217, was
originally a place to buy goats.

Broqueta de llagostins

(Prawn skewers with paprika)

These spiked delights should probably be in the pintxos section of this chapter, but we felt they were big enough to look after themselves. Just as there are two words for these crustaceans in English — *prawn* for the large version, and *shrimp* for the small version — so there are two words in Catalan: *llagostin* for the biggie, *gamba* for the littlie. For this recipe, you should definitely use *llagostins*.

2 garlic cloves, finely chopped

1 teaspoon cumin seeds, ground

2 generous pinches of smoked paprika

2 oregano sprigs, leaves picked and chopped

2 tablespoons olive oil

zest and juice of 1 large lemon

sea salt and freshly ground black pepper

12 large raw prawns (shrimp)

chilli flakes, for sprinkling

To make the marinade, combine the garlic, cumin, paprika, oregano, olive oil, lemon zest and lemon juice in a bowl. Season with salt and pepper and whisk until amalgamated.

Peel and devein the prawns, leaving the tails on. Add them to the marinade and leave for 20 minutes.

Thread the prawns onto four skewers, then grill (broil) or barbecue them over medium–high heat for 2 minutes on each side, brushing with the marinade.

Serve warm, with a sprinkling of chilli flakes.

Finocchi gratinati *(Baked fennel)*

Fennel was a familiar favourite for the ancient Greeks and Romans, because it is native to the western Mediterranean. The Greeks called the plant 'marathon', not because it lasts a long time but because it grew in profusion near the town that gave its name to the running race. Fennel is at its best in winter, and while it tastes pretty good in a salad, it's much better when it's been subjected to high heat, to bring out the sugar.

1.5 kg (3 lb 5 oz) fennel
sea salt and freshly
* ground black pepper*

80 ml (2½ fl oz/⅓ cup)
* olive oil*

2 tablespoons dry
* breadcrumbs*
2 tablespoons grated
* parmesan cheese*

Preheat the oven to 180°C (350°F).

Clean the fennel and peel off the outer layers. Cut the bulb into segments, wash them, then place in a saucepan of boiling salted water for 8 minutes.

Drain the fennel segments, dry them well, then place in an oiled baking dish in a single layer. Season with salt and pepper, drizzle with most of the olive oil and toss them around a bit until nicely coated in the oil.

Tip the breadcrumbs into a wide shallow bowl. Mix in the parmesan and sprinkle the mixture all over the fennel. Sprinkle with a little more olive oil and bake for a further 15 minutes, until the crumbs have turned into a lovely golden crust.

Serve hot.

Carciofi fritti *(Fried artichokes)*

Romans believe fried artichokes are a Jewish speciality, to be consumed at Passover, and they call this dish *Carciofi alla giudia*. The Catalans make no such religious assumption, and eat the finest flowers of winter all day long (we had them for breakfast in Barcelona's Boqueria market).

The kind that grow in Liguria are particularly suited for frying (or even for eating raw), but if you can't find the small Ligurian variety, try to use only the first young globe artichokes of the season. Once they've become big and bloated, towards the end of winter, you'll have to rip off so many outer leaves it's hardly worth the trouble.

6 young artichokes
juice of 1 lemon
2 eggs
4 marjoram sprigs,
  leaves picked and
  chopped

sea salt
90 g (3¼ oz/1½ cups) dry
  breadcrumbs
1.5 litres (52 fl oz/6 cups)
  vegetable oil, for deep-
  frying

lemon or chilli sauce,
  to serve

Clean the artichokes as instructed on page 19, leaving about 2 cm (1 inch) of the stems peeled. Slice the artichokes into wedges about 5–6 mm (¼ inch) thick and place them immediately in a bowl of cold water acidulated with the lemon juice.

In a bowl, beat the eggs, the marjoram and a pinch of salt. Spread the breadcrumbs on a flat plate and place it near the eggs.

Drain the artichokes and dry with paper towel. Dip the wedges into the egg mix, coating well, then roll them in the breadcrumbs, pressing hard until they are fully covered.

Pour the vegetable oil into a large saucepan and place over medium–high heat. When the oil is hot, fry the artichokes for 3–4 minutes, until golden brown. It is important that the artichokes are cooked through, as they will be bitter if underdone.

Drain on paper towel and serve hot, with some lemon wedges, or a chilli sauce if you prefer — or any of the garlic sauces from page 53 …

Note: If you'd like an improvement to this already wonderful recipe, think parmesan cheese. Take 25 g (1 oz/¼ cup) grated parmesan, put half of it in with the eggs, and sprinkle the remainder over the artichokes as a final flourish as they are served.

Artichauts aux petits pois

(Artichokes with peas)

Although artichokes were familiar to the ancient Romans, they don't seem to have become popular in France until the 15th century, when records started appearing of their planting near Avignon. Possibly they were rejected before then because the chefs had not cooked them for long enough, or had not thought to combine them with the sweetness of peas. Or perhaps the French disapproved of the way artichokes reduce the flavour of any wine that is drunk with them.

4 medium artichokes
125 ml (4 fl oz/½ cup)
* olive oil*
6–8 tiny white onions,
* skinned*
1 garlic clove, finely
* chopped*

50 g (1¾ oz) butter
250–300 g (9–10½ oz)
* small new potatoes,*
* washed and*
* thinly sliced*
300 g (10½ oz) fresh baby
* peas, shelled*

2 thyme sprigs
2 oregano sprigs
juice of ½ lemon
sea salt and freshly
* ground black pepper*

Clean the artichokes as instructed on page 19, keeping on about 2 cm (1 inch) of the stalks. Cut the artichokes into thin wedges.

Heat the olive oil in a non-stick — or preferably terracotta — pan over medium heat. Add the onions and sauté for about 6 minutes, until lightly golden. Add the garlic and stir for 2 minutes.

Add the butter and allow to melt, then add the artichokes and the potatoes. Cook for 4 minutes over medium heat, stirring.

When the potatoes and artichokes are coloured, pour in 500 ml (17 fl oz/2 cups) water and simmer, uncovered, for 15 minutes.

Add the peas, thyme and oregano. Cover the pan and cook on a low heat for a further 15 minutes, until the artichokes and potatoes are tender.

Stir the lemon juice through, season with salt and pepper and serve.

Artichauts à la barigoule

(Artichokes stuffed with herbs and garlic)

The name of this preparation of artichokes comes from the Provençal word for a kind of mushroom, *barigoule,* which is no longer part of the dish. The cooking method is similar to a Ligurian technique called *all'inferno* ('hell style'), because the artichokes are crammed into a baking dish and cooked in a hot oven, which reminds us of the damned souls reaching out from the underworld. Perhaps they have been condemned to hell for cannibalism, since part of the stuffing for the artichokes is artichoke stems.

6 globe artichokes, or 12 small ones
3 garlic cloves, finely chopped
15 g (½ oz/½ cup) finely chopped flat-leaf (Italian) parsley

4 marjoram sprigs, leaves picked and chopped
4 thyme sprigs, leaves picked and chopped
100 ml (3½ fl oz) olive oil

sea salt and freshly ground black pepper
2 white onions, finely chopped

Preheat the oven to 180°C (350°F). Cut off the stems of the artichokes, so the artichokes can sit upright; reserve the stems. Clean the flowers as instructed on page 19, then peel the stems to the tender heart.

Gently press each artichoke heart, top side down, on a chopping board, forcing the leaves apart to make them easier to stuff.

Finely chop the artichoke stems and place in a bowl. Add the garlic, parsley, marjoram and thyme. Stir a tablespoon of the olive oil into the mix and season with salt and pepper. Mix thoroughly.

In a non-stick frying pan over medium heat, cook the onion in a tablespoon or two of the olive oil for 5 minutes, stirring constantly. Remove from the heat and set aside.

Place the artichokes in an oiled baking dish, in a line, with their leaves facing up. Spoon the garlic mixture into each cavity. Scatter the onion around the artichokes. Pour water into the pan to reach about one-quarter of the way up the artichokes. Pour the remaining olive oil on and around the artichokes, then sprinkle with salt.

Bake for 40 minutes, by which time the sauce should be well reduced. Serve them warm, not too hot.

Artichokes are native to the Mediterranean and were seen as an aphrodisiac by the Greeks and the Romans, though connoisseurs of wine would disagree.

**ARTICHOKES WITH
HAM & PINE NUTS**
Recipe page 113

STUFFED ARTICHOKES
Recipe page 109

ARTICHOKES WITH PEAS
Recipe page 108

BARCELONA (CATALUNYA):
The Catalan name is *carxofa*,
the Ligurian is *carciofo*, and
the Provençal is *artichaut*.

Carxofes amb pernil

(Artichokes with ham and pine nuts)

Now we come to the Catalan approach to the flower that gets its name from the Arabic term *al khurshuuf*, which suggests the Moors introduced it to this part of the Mediterranean. It turns out that the saltiness of Spanish jamón (called *pernil* by the Catalans) creates a perfect partnership with the earthiness of artichokes.

8 artichokes
1½ lemons, cut in half
a handful of rock salt
100 ml (3½ fl oz)
   olive oil

4 garlic cloves,
   roughly chopped
3 tablespoons
   pine nuts

150 g (5½ oz) jamón or
   prosciutto, thickly sliced,
   then cut into strips
sea salt and ground white
   pepper

Clean the artichokes as instructed on page 19, cut them into quarters, then use a teaspoon or a small sharp knife to scoop out the hairy chokes. Place them immediately in a bowl of cold water acidulated with the juice of 1 lemon.

Bring a large pot of water to the boil, then add a small handful of rock salt and the juice of the remaining lemon half. Add the artichokes and simmer for about half an hour, until tender.

In the meantime, heat the olive oil in a large pan, preferably terracotta, over medium heat. When hot, add the garlic and the pine nuts and stir around for 2 minutes, taking care not to let the garlic burn.

Now you can add the jamón or the prosciutto and some freshly ground white pepper to taste. Mix thoroughly and cook, stirring, for 3 minutes.

Add enough of the artichoke cooking water to cover. Cook for 1 minute, then drain the artichokes and add them to the pan. Sauté gently over a low heat for 10 minutes, shaking the pan regularly — do not stir any more.

Your *carxofes* are now ready. You can eat them hot or cold, as a side, as a starter, as a light lunch, or as a wonderful tapas with an aperitif or a glass of white wine.

Carpaccio alla capponada

(Salmon carpaccio with anchovy salad)

Carpaccio is a much abused term in modern restaurants. The dish was originally made with raw beef, and in the early 1960s Harry's Bar in Venice named it in honour of the deep red colouring in the paintings of Vittore Carpaccio, who died in 1526 without ever eating the dish that took his name. Nowadays the term has been extended to include any raw ingredient, which means it is applied to the sliced raw seafood that used to be known as crudo. For this appetiser, we've paired the raw fish (more pink-coloured than Carpaccio-scarlet) with a classic Ligurian crunchy-bread salad.

300 g (10½ oz) sashimi-grade salmon, swordfish or tuna, in one piece
18 green olives, pitted and roughly chopped
6 anchovy fillets, chopped
1 teaspoon salted capers, rinsed and dried
1 teaspoon finely chopped oregano
1 teaspoon red wine vinegar
2 tablespoons olive oil
2 slices of Italian bread
1 garlic clove, finely chopped
juice of 1 lemon
sea salt and freshly ground black pepper

Preheat the oven to 180°C (350°F).

Thinly slice the fish and arrange on four plates. In a bowl, place the olives, anchovies, capers and oregano. Mix with the vinegar and a tablespoon of the olive oil.

Cut the bread into small cubes and place in a small bowl. Add the garlic and a splash of olive oil and mix well. Place on a baking dish and bake for about 2 minutes on each side, until crispy. Drizzle the lemon juice over the fish, then the remaining olive oil.

Arrange the caper and olive mixture on top of the fish. Scatter the bread on top, season with salt and pepper and serve.

CAMOGLI (LIGURIA): The town's name, *Camuggi* in local dialect, translates as 'house of wives', who were presumably waiting for their seafaring husbands.

Cuculli Genovesi

(Potato and pine nut fritters)

These little croquettes, a specialty of eastern Liguria, seemed to us to be an ideal addition to any tapas spread (or a pintxos spread, since they are eminently stab-able with toothpicks). The word *cuculli* is slang for 'hyperactive children', and the theory is these dumplings will calm them down more effectively than any drug. Often *cuculli* are made with chickpea flour, but Lucio's mother preferred to use potatoes.

1 kg (2 lb 4 oz) boiling potatoes, such as desiree or king edward
100 g (3½ oz) butter
4 marjoram sprigs, leaves picked and chopped

45 g (1½ oz/½ cup) grated parmesan
50 g (1¾ oz/⅓ cup) pine nuts, roughly crushed
sea salt
3 eggs

45 g (1½ oz/⅓ cup) dry breadcrumbs
olive oil, for deep-frying

Wash the potatoes, place in a saucepan and cover with cold water. Bring to the boil, then simmer over medium heat for about 20 minutes, or until tender. Drain and leave until cool enough to peel, then put them in a bowl and mash with a potato masher or ricer. Cut the butter into small pieces and add to the potatoes. Mix with a wooden spoon.

Continuing to work the mixture, add the marjoram, parmesan, pine nuts and a few pinches of salt. Separate the eggs and add the yolks, one at a time, mixing vigorously to amalgamate well and obtain a soft and creamy mixture. Using two spoons, form into balls the size of walnuts.

Pour the breadcrumbs onto a large plate. Whisk the egg whites together, for dipping the dumplings into.

Pour the olive oil into a frying pan, to a depth of about 5 cm (2 inches) and place over high heat. Let the oil get very hot — 190–200°C (375–400°F) if you have a thermometer — or otherwise drop a piece of bread into the oil, and if it sizzles right away it is ready.

Roll the *cuculli* first in the egg white, then in the breadcrumbs, and fry in the hot oil a few at a time for about 3 minutes, until they are golden brown on all sides. They will fluff up a little and become soft.

Drain briefly on paper towel. Serve hot, sprinkled with salt.

Note: Instead of frying them, you can bake the *cuculli* on a greased baking tray for 5 minutes in a preheated 200°C (400°F) oven. Either way they must be served very hot.

Salads

SAN FRUTTUOSO (LIGURIA):
The abbey and beach, near the
fashionable village of Portofino, can
only be reached by boat or foot.

Cool, fresh and seasoned

The word 'salad' came into English in the 14th century, derived from the Provençal word salada, *which in turn developed from the Latin word for salt.*

The Ligurian word *insalata* has the same origin. But the Catalan term for salad is *amanida*, which means 'seasoned'.

Nothing in the word's origin implies greens, or rawness, or cold, or fresh — so a salad can pretty much include any ingredient that might benefit from a dressing. But once you start labelling a salad as the signature of a particular region, you need to play by the rules, or risk being accused of salad-abuse.

In Liguria, for example, restaurants offer a dish they call *Insalata Catalana*, containing cold poached seafood with fresh greens, pickled vegetables and complex dressings. A dish like that is rarely seen in Catalunya, where the standard *amanida* avoids such opulent ingredients as lobster or scampi. If a Catalan salad contains protein at all, it is likely to be sliced ham, anchovies or tinned tuna. In this chapter, we're calling *Insalata Catalana* (page 133) a Ligurian speciality.

The American food scholar Colman Andrews has discerned these four rules for salad making in Catalunya: the best 'seasoning' is simply oil and salt; it's okay to put a little vinegar on onions, but never on tomatoes or meats or fish; the ingredients should not be mixed or tossed together, only layered on each other; and slightly green and firm tomatoes are better than ripe ones. The exception is *Xatonada* (page 137), where the salad was an afterthought, constructed to go with a wonderful sauce.

The Provençals take salad making more seriously than the Catalans, and the pinnacle of their efforts is of course *Salade Niçoise* (page 124), which has 12 ingredients in its most basic form, before you even think of adding such Parisian 'improvements' as potatoes and green beans.

Niçoise is the most abused salad in history. Provençal chef Jacques Médecin once declared: 'All over the world, horrified, I have seen the remains of other people's meals being served under the name Salade Niçoise.' (Médecin, whose encyclopedia of Provençal cooking contains 300 recipes, was an expert on fraud — he spent years in jail for tax evasion while Mayor of Nice.)

Ligurians have their own versions of Niçoise that they call either *capponada* or *condiggion*, but the pinnacle of their salady endeavours is *Cappon magro* (page 128), a construction of at least 12 types of vegetables and seafood, which has been described as more a work of architecture than of cuisine.

The Catalans would approve of the fact that *Cappon magro* is layered, not tossed, but horrified by its dressing of salsa verde (seven ingredients by itself). Ligurians might respond that the salsa verde is not so much a dressing as a glue that holds the structure together!

Salade Niçoise

This is a late-summer salad that makes an entire meal. It seemed to originate simultaneously in the south-east of France and the north-west of Italy during the 19th century, but since then it has been much abused as it spread throughout the world. The American food scholar Waverley Root, writing after a tour of Provence in 1958, had some shocking news for thousands of modern chefs: 'A genuine salade Niçoise should contain nothing cooked, with the possible exception of hard-boiled egg, a rather dubious addition not often permitted in Nice itself … In Paris I have been served a so-called salade Niçoise containing cooked string beans and even potatoes, necessarily cooked, but a purist would regard either of these, particularly the last, with horror.' Waverley Root also disapproves of the use of lettuce in a true Niçoise.

The Ligurians do a similar salad they call *condiggion* or *capponada*. They add garlic-rubbed toast, capers and fresh oregano to the basic Niçoise — but no potatoes, no beans and no mustard. They use raw capsicums (bell peppers), which are missing from most French versions.

Our recipe gives you the choice of being a Provençal purist or a Parisian potato-head. Let's call this a Ligurianised Niçoise.

1 small red onion, thinly sliced
8 small potatoes, halved (optional)
4 eggs (optional)
150 g (5½ oz) small green beans (optional)
1 red capsicum (bell pepper)
1 yellow capsicum (bell pepper)
16 small black olives, pitted (Taggiasca or Niçoise would be best)
4 very ripe tomatoes

2 Lebanese (short) cucumbers
2 sashimi-quality tuna steaks, or 300 g (10½ oz) best-quality tinned tuna in olive oil
2 baby cos (romaine) lettuce
a handful of basil leaves, torn
10 brown anchovy fillets (see page 19), drained
sea salt and freshly ground black pepper

Dressing
1 garlic clove, crushed
5 basil leaves, torn
2 brown anchovy fillets (see page 19), drained
sea salt and freshly ground black pepper
100 ml (3½ fl oz) olive oil
1 tablespoon red wine vinegar
1 tablespoon dijon mustard (optional)

For the dressing, place the garlic, basil and anchovy fillets in a mortar with a pinch of salt. Pound until you have a paste. Transfer to a bowl and add the olive oil, vinegar and the mustard, if you're using it. Whisk thoroughly. Grind in a little pepper.

Place the thinly sliced onion in a small bowl. Sprinkle with 3 tablespoons of the dressing and leave to marinate while you're doing the other steps, to take some of the bite out of them.

If you're using the potatoes, boil them in salted water for 10 minutes, then drain and set aside.

If you're using the eggs, boil them for 8 minutes, remove from the hot water and plunge them into cold water. Peel the eggs and cut them into wedges. Set aside.

If you're using green beans, top and tail them, then boil them in salted water for 6 minutes. Drain, then plunge them into icy water so they stop cooking and stay crunchy. Set aside.

Trim the capsicums, discarding the seeds and membranes, and finely slice them. Set aside.

If the olives have their stones, squash the olives with the side of a large knife, and pull the pips out.

Skin and seed the tomatoes, then slice them into quarters. Cut the cucumbers in half and, with a teaspoon, scoop out and discard the seeds. Cut into small half-moons and set aside.

Brush both sides of the tuna steaks with olive oil. Sear them in a hot non-stick frying pan for 2 minutes on each side (or a little longer if you prefer it well done). Transfer the steaks to a plate and let them rest for 5 minutes.

Arrange the leaves of the lettuce hearts on a large serving dish. Sprinkle with a bit of the remaining dressing. Cut the tuna into 2 cm (½ inch) chunks, and place half the chunks onto the lettuce leaves.

Into another bowl, place the marinated onion slices, olives, basil and all the vegetables. Dress with half of the remaining dressing and mix thoroughly. Layer this mixture on top of the tuna on the lettuce leaves, then top with the remaining tuna.

Arrange the egg wedges and the anchovies on top, sprinkle with the rest of the dressing and serve.

SALADE NIÇOISE
Recipe page 124

CAPPON MAGRO
Recipe page 128

Cappon magro

(Riviera seafood spectacular)

CINQUE TERRE
Serves 4 as a
complete meal,
or 8 as part
of a banquet

This is a complicated dish, which you're unlikely to make more than once a year, and then only if you have very important guests to entertain. In the 19th century, it was designed to celebrate the return of the Ligurian sailors after months at sea, when their wives would attempt to include every ingredient they could get their hands on, from the sea and from the land. The name *cappon magro* seems to mean 'skinny chicken', which is an ironic way to describe a very fat seafood and vegetable salad.

The recipe you're about to read, believe it or not, is a simplified version. The full *cappon magro* was served on hard ship's biscuits (which we've replaced with toasted bread) and formed a pyramid of seafood and raw and cooked vegetables, topped with a lobster, which sat in the middle of the table for guests to help themselves.

If you want to be closer to the traditional presentation, add a halved poached lobster and two dozen oysters to the feast. But you may find this version is enough.

about 500 ml (17 fl oz/ 2 cups) olive oil, for dressing and cooking all the various ingredients
sea salt

For the vegetables
300 g (10½ oz) potatoes, peeled and cut into slices about 1 cm (½ inch) thick
½ small cauliflower, cut into 8 florets
300 g (10½ oz) carrots, cut into thin discs
300 g (10½ oz) green beans, trimmed and cut into 5 cm (2 inch) pieces

For the poaching liquid
5 bay leaves
1 small carrot, cut into quarters
a splash of white wine

For the seafood
500 g (1 lb 2 oz) skinless white fish fillets, such as john dory or whiting
8 medium raw prawns (shrimp)
8 scampi or crayfish
8 mussels, scrubbed clean, beards removed
8 clams (vongole), scrubbed

For the salad
8 thin slices ciabatta bread, toasted
1 tablespoon white wine vinegar
200 g (7 oz) Salsa verde (page 41)
2 celery hearts, cut into thin discs
8 gherkins (pickles)
½ lemon
8 anchovy fillets
2 tablespoons capers, rinsed and dried
2 tablespoons pine nuts

To garnish (optional)
a handful of black olives
a handful of green olives
16 champignons, in oil

Boil all the vegetables separately — the potatoes and cauliflower for about 15 minutes, carrots about 10 minutes, and the beans for about 5 minutes. Drain well, refresh in iced water, then drain again. Dress them with a splash of the olive oil and a sprinkling of salt and set them aside.

Prepare the fish poaching liquid by adding the bay leaves and carrot to a saucepan of water. Bring to the boil, add a splash of white wine, then add the fish fillets and poach for 6 minutes. Let them cool in the water, then remove the fillets and dress them with some more of the olive oil. Set aside.

In the same poaching water, poach the prawns and scampi for 4 minutes, then remove from the water and set aside.

Cook the mussels and clams in a covered pan over high heat for 5 minutes, until they open, and set them aside.

Now we start layering the salad. Cover the bottom of a wide, deep serving dish with the toasted bread slices. Sprinkle the slices with the vinegar and a little olive oil. Spread about ½ teaspoon of salsa verde over each bit of toast, then top them with the sliced potatoes. Spread salsa verde over the potatoes, then top them with half the fish fillets, then more salsa verde, then the carrots, more sauce, the beans, more sauce, the rest of the fish, the celery hearts and finally another layer of sauce.

Now decorate the top with the prawns, the scampi and the gherkins. Squeeze the juice from the half lemon over it all.

Arrange the cauliflower florets around the salad, topping each floret with an anchovy.

Arrange the opened mussels and clams around the cauliflower.

If you don't think that's enough, arrange green and black olives and the mushrooms around the shellfish. Sprinkle the capers and pine nuts over everything.

Let the salad rest for 20 minutes, then serve this little piece of Ligurian history in the middle of the table for your guests to help themselves to. Or you could serve the salad as individual portions, as we did in our photo on page 127.

Marvels in marble

Around 600 BC, a small band of Greeks built one of their trading posts on a bay in north-west Italy they named Selene, after their moon goddess. The Romans arrived around 200 BC, pacified the local Liguri tribe, changed the bay's name to Luna, and made it a naval base (from which they sailed across to Spain). They terraced the surrounding hills to create olive groves, and planted chestnut forests to feed future armies.

Beside the bay they used marble from the Carrara mountains to build a city so magnificent it was sacked several times by marauding barbarians, who thought they had reached Rome. Every time, Luna rebuilt itself. When the Roman empire collapsed, the local Christians stripped off the marble to create façades for their churches, and changed the name from Luna to Luni.

An earthquake knocked many of the buildings down, the bay silted up and the citizens moved up into the hills to escape a malaria plague. Luni is now just an amphitheatre and an archeological dig, which has unearthed a magnificent mosaic of a boy riding a dolphin.

While Luni sank, Carrara thrived. In the 14th century Dante took shelter there while on the run from corrupt politicians in Florence. In the 15th century, Michelangelo sourced marble there for his statues and monuments, and built a system of roads to shift the marble blocks down the hill, so he could ship them to Rome. While living in Carrara, Michelangelo scribbled what looks like menus for dinner parties, including references to herrings, anchovies, fennel, ravioli, and soup made with the ancient grain farro.

Nowadays Carrara continues to boom. The marble extracted from the quarries earns Italy about €330 million a year. Much of it is sold to Muslim countries for the construction of mosques.

A ten-minute drive from the Luni ruins is a restaurant called Capannina Ciccio, which was founded by Lucio's mother, father, uncle and aunt in 1950, and is now run by Lucio's cousin Mario Guelfi. From its verandah, you can look across the Magra River to the marble mountains of Carrara. Ciccio specialises in whole baked local fish, but one of its signature starters is a farro soup that's not far from what Michelangelo would have eaten. Ciccio also offers a seafood soup called *cacciucco* that's pretty close to *bouillabaisse* and *sarsuela*.

The anchovies Michelangelo loved were caught near the five fishing villages known as the Cinque Terre. The villages snuggle into clefts between steep cliffs, and the cliffs are laced with terraces on which grapes were grown for wine. Many of the grape terraces are now abandoned. Climbing these cliffs, even with the help of donkeys or the monorail, is just too hard.

CARRARA (TUSCANY): The marble from these mountains was used for the Roman city of Luni and, 1500 years later, for the sculptures of Michelangelo.

Insalata Catalana di gamberi

(Prawn and celery salad)

A seafood salad labelled 'Catalana' is found on menus all along the Ligurian coast, displaying what Ligurian chefs imagine to be a favourite of their Catalan cousins. Its ingredients vary according to the pretensions of the restaurant serving it — those with wealthy clients might include lobster, crab and scampi. We decided to show you the simplest possible version, and then move on to a genuine Catalan salad, which the Catalans call *Salpicon de marisco* (page 134).

20 medium raw prawns (shrimp)
3 celery hearts, with leaves, sliced thinly

1 red onion, sliced very thinly
20 cherry tomatoes, quartered

olive oil, for drizzling
juice of 1 lemon
sea salt and freshly ground black pepper

Add the whole prawns to a saucepan of boiling salted water and cook for 2 minutes, then scoop them out and set aside in a bowl.

Place the vegetables in a large bowl and dress them with olive oil and lemon juice. Toss them thoroughly and leave to marinate while finishing the prawns.

When the prawns have cooled, peel and devein them, discarding the shells, but keeping the heads and putting them back into the bowl you kept the prawns in.

Place the vegetable salad in a large serving dish. Arrange the prawns on top.

Squash the prawn heads with a wooden spoon to push out their juices. Pour the juice over the prawns, sprinkle with salt and pepper and serve.

Salpicon de marisco *(Seafood salad)*

This dish started in Andalucia, then spread north to the Costa Brava. The Spanish word *salpicon* just means 'mixture', and there are no strict rules about what seafood must be included. This can be part of a lavish antipasto on a summer's day, or a main course any time of the year. The seafood is diced, sometimes very finely, then bound with a dressing. It can also be used as a generous stuffing — for example, inside calamari.

This version is similar to the Ligurian *insalata di mare*, which Lucio's mother perfected while working in the kitchen at Ciccio's restaurant in Bocca di Magra. We're making the onion optional, for those who love raw onion, but we're suggesting you soften the flavour by soaking it in water for 10 minutes.

2 tablespoons olive oil

1 teaspoon vinegar
or lemon juice

300 g (10½ oz) baby
octopus, cleaned
and cut into
quarters

8 whole scampi
or crayfish

600 g (1 lb 5 oz) raw
prawns (shrimp)

600 g (1 lb 5 oz) black
mussels, scrubbed clean,
beards removed

250 g (9 oz) skinless
rockfish or other sweet
firm white fish fillets,
cut into chunks

12 iceberg lettuce leaves

crusty bread, to serve

For the vinaigrette

1 white onion (optional)

1 small red capsicum
(bell pepper)

1 small green capsicum
(bell pepper)

80 ml (2½ fl oz/⅓ cup)
olive oil

30 ml (1 fl oz) white wine
vinegar or lemon juice

sea salt and freshly
ground black pepper

Bring a saucepan of salted water to a simmer. Add 1 tablespoon of the oil, the vinegar and baby octopus and simmer for 30 minutes. Remove from the heat, let the octopus cool down in the water, then drain and set aside.

In a clean pan of boiling water, cook the scampi for 3 minutes. Lift the scampi out and set it aside. In the same water, cook the whole prawns for 3 minutes, then remove and set aside.

Put the mussels in a clean pan with a little fresh water over medium heat. Cover and cook for about 6 minutes, tossing them now and then, and pulling them out as the shells open. Set them aside in a bowl, with the water they have expelled.

Heat the remaining tablespoon of oil in a frying pan over medium heat. Sear the rockfish pieces for 2 minutes each side. Remove from the pan and set aside.

While the seafood is simmering, prepare the vinaigrette. If you're planning to include the onion, cut it in half, leave it in cold water for 10 minutes, then dry it and finely dice. Halve the capsicums, discarding the stalks, seeds and membranes. Slice them lengthways into thin strips, then crossways into dice.

Pour the olive oil and vinegar into a large bowl, whisk to amalgamate, then add the capsicum and diced onion, if using. Season with salt and pepper and mix together.

Take the mussels out of their shells and place in a large bowl. Peel the scampi and the prawns, slice them into small pieces and add them to the mussels. Add the octopus and rockfish pieces. Pour three-quarters of the dressing over the seafood and mix thoroughly but gently. Now let the mixture rest for half an hour.

Arrange the salpicon on a large platter and drizzle with the rest of the dressing.

Serve in the middle of the table, with about three lettuce leaves per guest, and surrounded by plenty of bread, so they can scoop the salad into their lettuce cups and dip their bread into the juices.

Three salt cod winter salads

Remojon
(Salad of salt cod, oranges and black olives)

The winter salad called *remojon* may seem a strange combination of fruit and raw fish, but the flavour hit is sensational. It uses baccala — dried salt cod — which needs to be soaked for 48 hours to remove most of the salt. You could then bake or boil the baccala, but we're suggesting you leave it raw, so its earthiness matches the bittersweet oranges and the sourness of the onion. The dressing should just be a rich and fruity olive oil.

250 g (9 oz) baccala (dried salt cod)
3 oranges
1 white onion, finely sliced
olive oil, for drizzling
a handful of black olives, pitted
sea salt and freshly ground black pepper
2 pinches of smoked paprika

Soak the baccala for 48 hours, changing the water four times a day, and leaving it in the fridge the rest of the time. Skin the baccala and carefully remove the bones. Shred the flesh into small pieces and set aside.

Peel the oranges and slice each one into about eight pieces, removing all the white pith. Compose them in a bowl, with the onion slices. Sprinkle with a little olive oil and scatter the baccala over the top.

Season with salt, pepper and the paprika. Splash on more olive oil as you are serving.

Esqueixada *(Salad of salt cod and tomatoes)*

If you replace the oranges in the *Remojon* recipe with tomatoes, you get another salad called *esqueixada*, which means 'shredded' (what you do with the baccala). Purists declare this must be done with your hands, but we're willing to let you use a fork as well as your fingers.

Because the tomatoes lack the sweetness of the oranges, you could intensify the experience by dressing the *esqueixada* with a mixture of olive oil and sherry vinegar.

250 g (9 oz) baccala (dried salt cod)
3 tomatoes, peeled, seeded and diced
1 white onion, finely sliced (optional)

a handful of black olives, pitted
sea salt and freshly ground black pepper
2 pinches of smoked paprika (optional)

For the dressing
80 ml (2½ fl oz/⅓ cup) olive oil
1 tablespoon sherry vinegar

Soak the baccala for 48 hours, changing the water four times a day, and leaving it in the fridge the rest of the time. Skin the baccala and carefully remove the bones. Shred the flesh into small pieces and set aside.

Compose the tomatoes in a bowl, with the onion if you're using it. Whisk together the dressing ingredients, then sprinkle half of it over the tomatoes and scatter the baccala over the top. Season with salt and pepper, and paprika if you like a little spice. Splash on more of the dressing just as you are serving.

Xatonada *(Curly endive and salt cod salad)*

Here is another salt cod salad called *xatonada*, which is an excuse to use *xató*, the wonderful sauce from chapter 2. It's a speciality of southern Catalunya, spurring great rivalry between various villages that claim to have invented it. Because it contains two types of fish, this salad is traditionally served before Lent, to enable the devout to power up on protein before their 40 days of self-restraint on vegetables and sweets.

200 g (7 oz) baccala (dried salt cod)
1 large curly endive
3 teaspoons olive oil
1 teaspoon white wine vinegar

sea salt and freshly ground black pepper
150 g (5½ oz) best-quality tuna in oil
12 anchovy fillets
a handful of black olives

a handful of green olives
250 ml (9 fl oz/1 cup) Xató sauce (page 61)
Romesco sauce (page 44), to serve (optional)

Soak the baccala for 48 hours, changing the water four times a day, and leaving it in the fridge. Skin the cod, carefully remove the bones, then shred the flesh with a fork.

Break up the endive and wash the leaves, using just the beautiful yellow ones. Dry them in a spinner. Place in a large bowl and sprinkle with the olive oil, vinegar, salt and pepper. Toss the leaves, then arrange on a large serving platter. Compose the shredded cod on the leaves. Top with the tuna, anchovies, olives and pine nuts.

Spoon a generous amount of xató sauce over the salad (or use half xató and half romesco for colour). Serve with slices of toasted bread, rubbed with garlic. Leave a bowl of xató sauce (and, if you like, some romesco too) on the table for your guests.

XATONADA:
BACCALA WITH CURLY ENDIVE
Recipe page 137

REMOJON:
BACCALA WITH ORANGES
Recipe page 136

**ESQUEIXADA:
BACCALA WITH TOMATOES
& SHERRY VINEGAR**
Recipe page 137

*The Greeks, the Romans and the Arabs all made their
contribution to the cuisine of the western Mediterranean,
and now it's time to meet the Vikings. Instead of pillaging
and conquering, they brought baccala — dried salt cod.
And the locals applied their ingenuity to preparing it.*

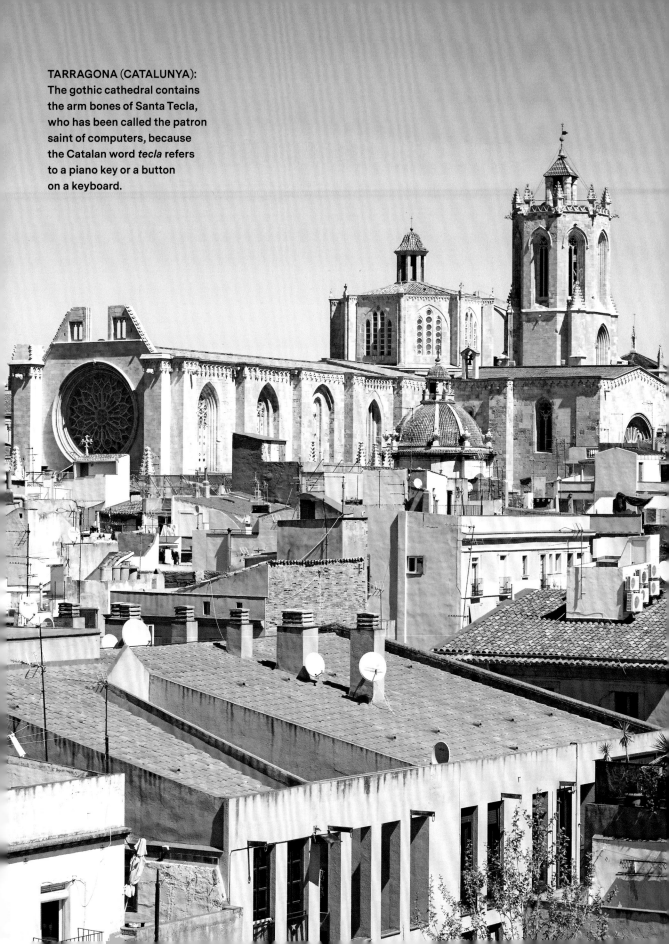

TARRAGONA (CATALUNYA):
The gothic cathedral contains
the arm bones of Santa Tecla,
who has been called the patron
saint of computers, because
the Catalan word *tecla* refers
to a piano key or a button
on a keyboard.

Escalivada *(Roasted vegetables)*

Ligurians would call this Catalan favourite a brilliant antipasto. The word *escalivada* means 'burnt in hot ashes' — or wood-fire barbecued, as modern chefs would say. We're letting you use an oven or a grill (broiler).

It's basically grilled vegetables, sliced and dressed with oil, garlic and salt, and served at room temperature with plenty of bread. We think you should spread marinated goat's cheese on the bread before piling on the vegies, so we've explained how to marinate the cheese at the end of the recipe. Or you could serve them with any of the sauces in chapter 2.

4 medium eggplants (aubergines)	4 large ripe tomatoes	olive oil, for drizzling
4 red capsicums (bell peppers)	3 spring onions (scallions), or 2 leeks, if they are in season	3 garlic cloves
		sea salt and freshly ground black pepper

Preheat the oven to 200°C (400°F). Wash and dry the eggplants, capsicums, tomatoes and spring onions (or leeks). Slice them in half, keeping the seeds and membranes in the capsicums.

Rub each vegetable with oil. Arrange the vegetables on a baking tray. If you're not keen on raw garlic, leave the garlic cloves whole and unpeeled and add them to the baking tray. Sprinkle the vegies with salt and a little olive oil.

Bake for 45 minutes, then cover with foil and bake for another 10 minutes. Remove from the oven and let the vegies cool under the foil.

Peel, seed and core the capsicums. Peel the other vegetables, then cut all the vegetables into strips, placing them in a bowl. Sprinkle with salt and pepper, and pour over them any juice that remains in the baking tray.

If you're using raw garlic, peel the cloves and slice very thinly. If you baked the garlic cloves, pop them out of their skins.

Arrange the vegetable strips on a serving dish, alternating with the slices of raw garlic, or adding the baked garlic cloves to the dish. Sprinkle with a little olive oil, cover with the foil, and let the *escalivada* rest in the fridge overnight.

Half an hour before serving, remove from the fridge to return to room temperature. Serve with toasts, and marinated goat's cheese (see recipe below).

Goat's cheese: For a marinated goat's cheese to serve with *escalivada*, cut 300 g (10½ oz) goat's cheese into slices about 1 cm (½ inch) thick. Crush 10–15 black peppercorns in mortar. Layer the cheese into a jar, dressing each layer with some of the crushed pepper, roasted garlic, olives, chopped fresh red chilli and thyme. Fill the jar with olive oil to cover completely.

You can also do this with pecorino cheese; just cut it into cubes before layering it with the garlic, peppercorns and other aromatics.

TELLARO (LIGURIA): The English writer D.H. Lawrence lived in this fishing village and reported a local legend in which a giant octopus reached out of the ocean and rang the churchbell to warn of approaching pirates.

Chapter Five

PASTA E RISO / PÂTES ET RIZ /
FIDEUS I ARROS

Pasta & Rice

GENOA (LIGURIA):
The warm microclimate
means you can eat lunch
outside for nine months
of the year.

Not entirely Italian

Let us shock you. It seems likely that pasta, in the form we buy it today, was not introduced to Spain by Italians but rather by Arabs.

Those Arabs *did* come from Sicily, so we might still be able to call them Italians. But that's unlikely to offer much solace to outraged Ligurians, who tend to think of Sicilians as foreigners anyway.

The Romans were making a form of pasta before year zero, and no doubt it was part of the cooking in their naval base at Luna (see chapter 4). They'd roll out thin sheets of dough (usually made with eggs) and layer them with beef stew to create what today we would call lasagne. Or they'd slice them into ribbons to make what we now call tagliatelle. What these otherwise brilliant engineers lacked was the technology to make their pasta portable.

That breakthrough happened for the Arabs in Sicily around the 10th century. They made noodles with durum wheat (and no egg) and dried them in the sun, which was plentiful down there. Then they bundled up the sticks of what they called *itriya* and carried them around the Med as a trading product. Apparently they sold them to the Genoese (who then reverse-engineered the technology). The Arabs also took *itriya* to Spain, along with rice.

So we must thank the Arabs not just for laying the groundwork for paella but also for *fideua*, the Catalan way of using noodles — broken up into fragments and cooked in the stock, just like rice.

The French have never been big on either rice or pasta. Their rice industry didn't get started until the 18th century, in the swamps of the Camargue in northern Provence. The Camargue now produces a white rice that is useless for either paella or risotto, and a red version which Provençal restaurants sometimes mix with white rice for visual effect, but which doesn't have any particular taste.

We were hard pressed to find a great French rice recipe for this chapter, so in the end we put one in the dessert chapter — with cherries.

We had a little more luck finding a French use of pasta — the extraordinary dish called *Macaronade* (page 162), which was brought to south-western France by sailors from Naples. The people of Nice like to serve ravioli with the meat stew they call *daube*, while their neighbours, the Monégasques, fry their ravioli to make a dish called *barbajuan* (though Ligurians will tell you these tasty parcels are the same as their *gattafin*).

The Ligurians mostly use fresh pasta, the way the Romans did. The major modern remnant of the dried *itriya* those Arab Sicilians sold to the Genoese 900 years ago would be *trenette*, the square-edged noodles cooked with green beans and potatoes.

The rest of the best of pasta is here.

Fideua negra *(Black noodles with seafood)*

Fideua is a Catalan specialty of broken-up thin noodles (called *fideus* in Spain, and *spaghettini* in Italy), which are cooked as if they were rice for a paella or a risotto. This is a wonderful way to cook pasta, because its own starch will enrich the sauce. You should use only dry pasta from a packet — fresh egg pasta is too delicate and will disintegrate.

According to legend, fideua was invented in the 19th century by fisherfolk from the town of Gandia in the south of Spain, who could not get enough rice but had access to spaghetti. Gandia still has an annual fideua cooking contest — although the best fideua we found was in a restaurant called Cal Joan, in Tarragona, somewhat to the north of Valencia.

The most important detail for the recipe: you need a great fish stock. In this recipe we keep the stock very simple, to exalt the flavour of the prawns, but you could use the one in our paella recipe on page 152, keeping in mind that the quantity of stock should be double the quantity of pasta. We add the ink of the cuttlefish to produce a spectacular black colouring, but it's not essential. Instead of this brunette fideua, you can also make a beautiful blonde fideua, as we'll explain afterwards.

500 g (1 lb 2 oz) large raw prawns (shrimp)
olive oil, for pan-frying
2 spring onions (scallions), finely chopped, green leaves reserved
½ teaspoon sea salt
1 kg (2 lb 4 oz) cuttlefish, cleaned
1 red capsicum (bell pepper), cut into strips

4 garlic cloves, finely chopped
4 bay leaves
1 green capsicum (bell pepper), diced
4 large tomatoes, peeled, seeded and diced
1 tablespoon sweet chilli powder
100 ml (3½ fl oz) Picada (page 60)
500 g (1 lb 2 oz) spaghettini

3 teaspoons cuttlefish ink (you can buy a jar from your fishmonger, or use a cuttlefish ink sac)
3 flat-leaf (Italian) parsley sprigs, leaves picked and finely chopped
2 pinches of saffron threads
Allioli (page 53), to serve

First make the stock. Peel the prawns, reserving the heads and shells; devein the prawns and set aside. Put a stockpot over medium heat and cover the bottom with olive oil. When the oil is hot, add the prawn heads and shells and fry them for 3 minutes, squashing them down with a wooden spoon to extract the juices. When they start to change colour, add 2 litres (70 fl oz/8 cups) water and the green spring onion tops. Add the salt, turn the heat down and simmer for 30 minutes, scooping off any scum that appears on top. Leave the stock on low heat until it is time to add it to the other ingredients.

Cut the tentacles off the cuttlefish. Cover the bottom of a large ovenproof pan — a paella pan, if you have one — with olive oil over high heat and fry the tentacles for about 3 minutes. When they turn golden, take them out of the pan and set them aside, to be used as decoration later.

In the same pan, fry the red capsicum strips for 5 minutes, until they soften. Set them aside in a bowl, with a pinch of salt.

In the same pan, fry the prawns over medium heat for about 1 minute each side, until they change colour. Set them aside.

Now make the *sofregit*. Lower the heat under the pan, splash in a little olive oil, then add the chopped spring onions, the garlic and bay leaves. Fry, stirring, for 5 minutes, until the onion is softened. Add the green capsicum and fry for another 5 minutes, stirring and shaking the pan.

Cut the cuttlefish into thin strips and add them to the pan. Fry for about 2 minutes, until the cuttlefish becomes ivory white. Add the chopped tomatoes and fry for another 2 minutes. Now add the sweet chilli powder and the picada, stirring and cooking until the tomatoes have begun to dissolve.

Break the spaghettini strands into small fragments; in Catalunya, fideus comes in different sizes, so the length of the fragments is up to you. Turn up the heat, stir the pasta into the sauce and cook for 4 minutes. (Alternatively, you can toast the spaghettini fragments in a little oil over high heat for 3 minutes to make them crunchy, then stir them into the sauce.)

Strain the stock and pour it into the fideua, stirring well. Add the 3 teaspoons of cuttlefish ink (or more, if you like) — either from the jar, or by using a wooden spoon to push the ink sac of a cuttlefish through a fine-mesh strainer held over the bubbling pan. Add the parsley and saffron and stir gently. Leave to cook for 10 minutes or so over medium heat.

Meanwhile, preheat the oven to 180°C (350°F).

Check if there's enough salt in the fideua for your taste, give it a final stir, then top the fideua with the strips of red capsicum and the tentacles you cooked earlier. Place the pan in the oven and bake for 5 minutes, so the top starts to crisp up.

Place the fideua in the middle of the table, with a bowl of allioli on the side, so your guests can serve themselves.

Variations: Fideus rossetjats, which literally translates as 'blonde noodles', replaces the cuttlefish (and its ink) with chopped-up fish fillets or prawns (shrimp) or calamari. The 'blonde' refers to the golden colour of the noodles when they have been toasted in olive oil. It can be decorated with green peas as well as red capsicums (bell peppers).

Fideus a banda ('fideus apart') is a version in which a strongly flavoured rockfish is cooked in water to make the stock, then served as a separate dish to the noodles.

FIDEUA WITH SQUID INK
Recipe page 148

PAELLA DE MARISC
Recipe page 152

Paella de marisc *(Seafood paella)*

It's hard to mess up paella, as long as your seafood is fresh, your stock is strong and your rice is short. In this recipe we detail how to make a great seafood stock, but you can shortcut by buying 1.5 litres (52 fl oz/6 cups) commercial fish stock. You don't need the artificial colouring powder that restaurants sometimes use with paella — saffron and paprika are quite enough. You are aiming to achieve these three qualities: the rice should be slightly firm to the bite (what Italians call *al dente)*; the paella should be moist but not soupy (the correct ratio of rice to stock is one to three); and there should be a little crust of caramelised rice at the bottom, which the Catalans call *soccarat*.

16 raw prawns (shrimp)
sea salt
150 ml (5 fl oz) olive oil
8 scampi or crayfish,
* halved*
500 g (1 lb 2 oz) cuttlefish,
* cleaned and sliced*
24 mussels, scrubbed
* clean, beards removed*
24 clams (vongole)
1 small fennel bulb,
* trimmed and finely*
* chopped*
1 white onion, finely
* chopped*
1 red capsicum (bell
* pepper), finely chopped*

1 green capsicum
* (bell pepper), finely*
* chopped*
3 garlic cloves, finely
* chopped*
2 large tomatoes, grated
* to the skin*
1 tablespoon smoked
* paprika*
1 teaspoon finely chopped
* hot red chilli*
400 g (14 oz) short-grain
* white rice*
a pinch of saffron threads
150 g (5½ oz/1 cup) fresh
* shelled peas*
lemon wedges, to serve

For the fish stock
1.5 kg (3 lb 5 oz) clean
* fish bones and heads*
60 ml (2 fl oz/¼ cup)
* olive oil*
1 leek, pale part only,
* cut in half; plus a*
* handful of leek leaves*
* (from the top), chopped*
60 ml (2 fl oz/¼ cup)
* white wine*
1 carrot, cut into chunks
1 white onion, peeled
* and cut in half*
2 celery stalks, with
* leaves, cut into quarters*
5 cherry tomatoes

Remove the heads from most of the prawns, and add them to the seafood scraps for the stock (leave a few prawns whole to decorate the pan at the end).

To make the fish stock, wash the fish heads to get rid of any blood. Place a large saucepan over medium heat and splash the olive oil into it. When it's hot, add the bits of fish and fry them for about 5 minutes, squashing them with a wooden spoon to extract the juices. Add the leek leaves, fry for another minute, then pour in the wine. Stir and let the alcohol evaporate for 3 minutes. Add the rest of the vegetables, including the cherry tomatoes, and fill the pan near to the top with cold water.

Bring the mixture to the boil, then turn the heat down and let it simmer for at least 45 minutes. Skim any scum off the top. Strain the stock through a fine sieve, squashing some of the soft parts through the sieve with a wooden spoon. Reserve a few cups in a jar in the fridge to serve as an elegant consommé, and place the pan back over low heat until it's time to add it to the paella.

Put a paella pan (or a wide frying pan) over medium heat. When it's very hot, sprinkle a generous amount of salt over the base of the pan, then add enough olive oil to cover the surface. When it sizzles, brown the scampi and the prawns for 2 minutes each side, take them out and set them aside. Remove most of the scampi and most of the prawns from their shells and discard the shells. Leave a few cooked prawns and a few cooked scampi whole for decoration at the end.

Brown the cuttlefish for about 8 minutes, then take it out and put it with the prawns and scampi.

Put the mussels and clams in a covered pan with a little water over high heat. Cook them for about 3 minutes, until they start to open. Take most of them out of their shells and put them in the bowl with the prawns and other seafood. Keep a few in their shells for decoration. Discard the empty shells, but strain the liquid they have released into the stock.

Add the fennel, onion and capsicums to the paella pan and fry them for 5 minutes, then add the garlic and fry the mixture for 3 minutes more.

When the vegetables are soft, push them to the edge of the pan, and in the centre, add the tomatoes, paprika and chilli. Mix them and fry for 3 minutes, then stir the other vegetables through them. Add the browned cuttlefish and cook for another 3 minutes, stirring gently.

You have now created the *sofregit* in which the rice will cook. Scatter the rice around the pan and sprinkle the saffron on top. Stir the rice through the *sofregit* and let it absorb the flavours for 3 minutes.

Now pour in about 1.25 litres (44 fl oz/5 cups) of the warm fish stock. Mix, check to see if there's enough salt for your taste, then cook for 10 minutes over high heat, shaking the pan occasionally and moving it around over the heat source so the rice cooks evenly.

Add the prawns, the scampi, mussels, clams and the peas. Push them down into the rice without stirring. Try not to contact the bottom of the pan, because a little crust will be forming there. Arrange the prawns, scampi, mussels and clams that are still in their shells artistically over the top. Cook for another 5 minutes over medium heat.

Take off the heat, cover with a tea towel and let your paella rest for 5 minutes.

Serve it in the middle of the table with some lemon wedges on the side, for those who like to squeeze it over their food.

TARRAGONA (CATALUNYA):
The Romans named the settlement Tarraconensis, from a Phoenician word meaning 'citadel'. It became a resort town for the emperors, and by 200 AD the entertainment in the amphitheatre included the slaughter of Christians.

All roads lead to Tarragona

The citizens of sunny Tarragona, just south of Barcelona, are proud their town was established by Roman invaders around 200 BC, under the name Tarraconensis. Around the amphitheatre — where a local Christian bishop named Fructuosus was martyred by the Romans in 259 AD — they have planted the fruit trees (peach, pear and apricot) and fragrant herbs that the Romans would have consumed.

The signs explain: 'Roman agriculture was based on the Mediterranean trilogy: cereals (mainly wheat), vines and olives. From these they obtained flour and bread, grapes and wine, olives and olive oil — the basis of the Roman diet. Very aromatic plants were used to make perfumes and for various religious rituals. Thyme, for example, was burned to make holy smoke. Plums were eaten at funerary banquets. In a Roman house you would find rosemary, thyme, fennel, wormwood, ginger, marjoram and oregano, alongside vegetables and flowers such as roses, violets and hyacinths.' No doubt they were enjoyed by the emperors Augustus and Hadrian, who treated Tarraconensis as a holiday retreat.

The city was sacked by Vandals and Huns when the Roman empire collapsed, and the Arabs occupied it for 50 years, but by the 12th century it had become a thriving Christian metropolis, allocated its own patron saint — Tecla, a 1st-century woman who was condemned to death for fighting off a nobleman trying to rape her, but who was saved from every Roman attempt at execution by a series of miracles.

Towards the end of September, the Tarragonans celebrate her life with a week-long festival, and march through the Medieval quarter carrying giant statues of roosters with breasts and firework-spouting dragons. Presumably they represent the wild beasts that failed to kill her, in another of the miracles that justified her rise to sainthood. Tecla's arm is preserved in the gothic cathedral.

Tarragona's other claim to fame is the quality of its paella; Catalunya's rice fields are just to the south, producing the short-grain rice sometimes known as *arros redondo* or *bomba*. But it is also the home of Catalunya's best *fideua*, made with a local form of broken-up noodles called *fideus* — which the Italians would know as *fedellini*. The local taste for rice and pasta was inspired by the Arabs, and those traditions are treated with reverence in a restaurant called Cal Joan, in the docks area at the opposite end of the beach from the Roman amphitheatre.

Within what the locals call 'a formerly dubious tavern', Joan Cobos and his daughter Esther have been cooking superb seafood since 1997. And because this is Roman Tarraconensis, every table is set with a bowl of the city's signature sauce, romesco.

Pasta arrosto con le arselle

(Roasted spaghetti with baby clams)

In recent years, it has become fashionable in northern Italy to serve a dish called *pasta risottata*, which is similar to *fideua* in that noodles are cooked as if they are rice in risotto, rather than boiled in the usual way. We had assumed this was a new idea, possibly inspired by the Catalan *fideua*, but going through a Ligurian cookbook published in the early 1800s, we came across a fantastic recipe similar to *fideua* but much simpler, where the pasta is 'roasted' in the sauce. In spring you can add fresh peas, for colour and flavour.

1 kg (2 lb 4 oz) clams (vongole), pippies or cockles
100 ml (3½ fl oz) olive oil
a handful of finely chopped flat-leaf (Italian) parsley
1 garlic clove, chopped

5 tomatoes, peeled, seeded and diced
sea salt and freshly ground black pepper
40 g (1½ oz/¼ cup) pine nuts, lightly crushed in a mortar

100 g (3½ oz/⅔ cup) podded fresh peas
400 g (14 oz) spaghetti, broken into small pieces

Put the clams, with a little water, in a saucepan. Cover and place over high heat for about 3 minutes, until the clams start to open, removing them as they open. Strain the liquid into a bowl, keeping the saucepan handy. When the clams have cooled, take them out of their shells and set them aside in the bowl with the cooking water.

Preheat the oven to 180°C (350°F).

Splash the olive oil into the pan the clams were cooked in and place it over medium heat. Add the parsley and garlic; stir and sizzle for 3 minutes.

Add the tomatoes and a little salt and pepper, mixing thoroughly. Allow the sauce to reduce over medium heat for 6 minutes. Now add the pine nuts, the peas and the broken-up spaghetti. Stir and add the reserved water from the clams. Cook over medium heat for another 6 minutes, stirring regularly.

Stir in the clams, then spread the mixture over a baking tray or ovenproof frying pan. Bake for 10 minutes, until the pasta on the surface starts to turn golden.

Remove from the oven and leave to rest for 5 minutes before serving.

CAMOGLI (LIGURIA): During the Middle Ages it was one of the busiest ports of the Mediterranean; in the 1880 census, some 500 local citizens listed their occupation as 'ship captain'.

Paella Valenciana

(Chicken, rabbit and snail paella)

If you examine the ingredients list with this recipe, you'll see it starts with 18 snails. We don't actually expect you to include snails, but we thought you'd want to know what was in the original recipe for paella, which was created, as best we can establish, near Valencia in the 14th century.

The Moors brought rice to Spain in the 9th century, and by the 1300s the swamps inland from Valencia had become Spain's premier rice-growing region. For their own meals, the rice growers combined their harvest with the ingredients running around their feet — chickens, rabbits and snails (if 'running' is the appropriate word for what they do). The farmers spiced this rice stew with saffron, which the Greeks had brought to the area 1500 years earlier. When tomatoes and peppers took Spain by storm in the 16th century, they became essential ingredients in the dish that was named after the *patella*, the frying pan in which it was cooked, over an open fire.

18 snails (optional)
fine sea salt
185 ml (6 fl oz/¾ cup)
  olive oil, approximately
500 g (1 lb 2 oz) chicken
  pieces (ideally including
  6 drumsticks)
1 small rabbit, skinned
  and cut into 12 pieces
1 onion, chopped

1 garlic clove, chopped
5 tomatoes, skinned
  and seeded
1 generous teaspoon
  smoked paprika
1.5 litres (52 fl oz/6 cups)
  chicken stock
200 g (7 oz) fresh broad
  beans, peeled (out of
  season, use chopped

green beans, or peeled
  frozen broad beans)
200 g (7 oz) cooked or
  tinned borlotti beans
  or butterbeans
1 teaspoon saffron threads
500 g (1 lb 2 oz/2¼ cups)
  short-grain white rice
lemon wedges, to serve

In the unlikely event that you are using fresh snails, wash them well, boil them for 30 minutes and set them aside. Or open a tin of snails and drain them. Or skip this step.

Put a paella pan, or wide frying pan, over high heat and let it get very hot. Sprinkle with a generous amount of fine salt. Add a generous splash of olive oil, and when it is sizzling, add the chicken and rabbit pieces. (If your pan is not very big, work in two batches.) Brown the meat on all sides for about 15 minutes. Take out the meat and set aside.

Now make the *sofregit* (or use the version on page 49). Splash in more olive oil and sizzle the onion for 3 minutes. Add the garlic and stir gently for 1 minute. Add the tomatoes and cook for 3 minutes, then stir in the paprika.

Put the rabbit and chicken pieces back in the pan. Stir thoroughly and pour in the stock. Bring to the boil, then stir in the broad beans, borlotti beans and the snails, if you are using them. Add the saffron. When the mixture comes back to the boil, add the rice. Stir once and give the pan a shake to spread the rice evenly. Do not stir again.

Let the rice cook for 10 minutes over medium heat, never stirring, but moving the pan occasionally so the heat is under different parts of the pan. Reduce the heat to low and cook for another 6 minutes. Do not stir the paella. You want it to brown slightly at the bottom and form a crust.

Cover the pan and cook for another 5 minutes on very low heat. To check it is done, gently poke a spoon through the rice in the centre of the paella and look to make sure the rice is dry at the bottom. Allow to rest for 10 minutes.

Serve the paella in the middle of the table, with lemon wedges for squeezing over.

Macaronade *(Rigatoni with seafood sauce, mussels and stuffed calamari)*

This is a signature dish of Sète, a French port about halfway between Marseille and the Spanish border. As you stroll along the canal that runs through the middle of town, you pass bistro after bistro with a blackboard outside advertising its particular interpretation of a banquet that gets its name from the Italian word *macaroni* — the tube shape we call penne or rigatoni these days.

In one of these places, our macaronade consisted of 1) a bowl of penne in tomato and seafood sauce; 2) a bowl of stuffed mussels; 3) a plate of calamari rings in yellow batter; 4) a plate of stuffed calamari; 5) a plate of fried local cuttlefish called *seiche*; and 6) a bowl of French fries. We won't name the restaurant because the macaronade was not very good, but we were inspired to create our own simpler version.

We wondered how the French came to embrace macaroni, a specialty of southern Italy that is unknown in Liguria. The answer is that this dish is a legacy of the Italian workers and fishermen who arrived from Naples at the end of the 17th century to help build the Canal du Rhône, which connects to the Canal du Midi, north of Marseille.

Macaronade was a way to use up leftovers at the end of the week, with cheap cuts of meat and unsellable pieces of seafood. Now it's a Sunday lunch feast for friends and family. The recipe varies from family to family and restaurant to restaurant, but the secret is cooking the sauce for a long time to get the depth of flavour. Most often in Sète, you will find the mussels and calamari are stuffed with minced (ground) beef or pork, but we prefer the stuffing to be based on vegetables or seafood, because it is lighter.

Here we present macaroni with a seafood sauce, plus mussels and calamari as a side dish. You could serve it with a big bowl of chips, if you like — that would be suitably Sètoise. We prefer lots of crusty bread, to dip in the luscious sauce.

12 small stuffed calamari (from 'Parade of pintxos' on page 91)

500 g (1 lb 2 oz) cuttlefish, cleaned and thinly sliced

18 mussels, scrubbed clean, beards removed

500 g (1 lb 2 oz) penne or rigatoni

2 tablespoons non-egg Aïoli (see the variations on page 53)

crusty bread, to serve

Tomato sauce

80 ml (2½ fl oz/⅓ cup) olive oil

1 celery stalk, chopped

1 small carrot, chopped

½ white onion, finely chopped

2 garlic cloves, finely chopped

50 ml (1¾ fl oz) white wine

4 large tomatoes, peeled, seeded and chopped

sea salt and freshly ground black pepper

1 thyme sprig, leaves picked and chopped

6 basil leaves, roughly chopped

First, brown the stuffed calamari in a frying pan for 5 minutes on each side over medium–low heat. Remove from the pan and set aside.

Now brown the cuttlefish slices over high heat for about 3 minutes. Set aside.

To make the tomato sauce, heat the olive oil in a heavy-based saucepan over medium heat. Add the celery, carrot and onion and fry for 6 minutes, stirring now and then. Stir in the garlic and fry for 2 minutes. Add the wine and let the alcohol evaporate for 3 minutes.

Stir in the chopped tomatoes, then add the browned cuttlefish and fry for about 5 minutes. Season to taste with salt and pepper, add the thyme and basil, then stir in about 60 ml (2 fl oz/¼ cup) water.

Add the stuffed calamari and simmer, uncovered, for 10 minutes, shaking the pan regularly, and adding a little more water if it looks like drying out. Take the stuffed calamari out of the sauce and set aside.

Cook the mussels with a little water in a covered saucepan over high heat for about 5 minutes, until they all open. Set them aside, still in their shells, on a separate plate. Spoon a little of the tomato sauce into each mussel.

Meanwhile, boil the pasta for 3 minutes less than the time suggested on the packet. Drain the pasta, reserving about 60 ml (2 fl oz/¼ cup) of the cooking water.

Add the pasta and the cooking water to your big pot of tomato sauce and stir it through for 3 minutes over medium heat. You want the pasta to take on the red colour of the sauce. Gently stir the aïoli through the pasta, mixing thoroughly.

Transfer the pasta to a large serving plate, placing it in the middle of the table. Place the mussels and stuffed calamari in a bowl next to it. Supply lots of spoons and tongs so your guests can serve themselves, and offer lots of bread to slurp it all up with.

MACARONADE
Recipe page 162

**BEEF STEW
WITH RAVIOLI**
Recipe page 166

Daube de boeuf avec raviolis à la Niçoise / Ravioli di carne al tocco di carne *(Beef stew with ravioli)*

This is the meat lovers' special: beef-stuffed ravioli with a beef sauce.

The stew called *tocco di carne* is a favourite of eastern Liguria (the Levante) which somehow leapfrogged western Liguria (the Ponente) and arrived in Nice under an assumed name, *daube de boeuf.* The Niçois cooks (who might say the jump went the opposite way) also adopted ravioli from their neighbours, but made them smaller.

In Nice, this stew was traditionally cooked in a *daubière* — a heavy-bottomed jug with two handles and a concave lid (into which cold water is poured, so the steam condenses inside). The Ligurians settled for a standard terracotta cooking pot, which would have hung over the fire all day. You can also use a metal pot with a heavy bottom and a secure lid, as the meat must cook very slowly with no evaporating liquid.

The idea of beef stew with beef ravioli sounds pretty heavy for modern tastes, which is why we suggest you treat it as two meals. First, slow-cook your beef stew for at least 2 hours, and eat it with polenta or mashed potato, or the chickpea porridge called *Panisse* (page 190). Keep half the stew to make filling and sauce for the ravioli the next day.

For the daube
a handful of dried
  porcini mushrooms
  (30 g/1 oz)
600 g (1 lb 5 oz) chuck beef
60 ml (2 fl oz/¼ cup)
  olive oil
20 g (¾ oz) butter
50 g (1¾ oz) bone marrow
1 celery stalk, chopped
1 small carrot, chopped
1 white onion, chopped
1 garlic clove, chopped
3 bay leaves
100 ml (3½ fl oz) white
  wine, or red wine if
  you'd like a richer stew
5 ripe tomatoes, peeled
  and chopped (or a
  400 g/14 oz tin of
  crushed tomatoes)

sea salt and freshly
  ground black pepper
bouquet garni of
  Provençal herbs, such
  as fresh thyme and
  rosemary sprigs

For the pasta
4 eggs
400 g (14 oz/2⅔ cups)
  plain (all-purpose)
  flour, plus extra for
  dusting
sea salt

For the ravioli filling
45 ml (1½ fl oz) olive oil
1 garlic clove, chopped
1 tablespoon finely
  chopped flat-leaf
  (Italian) parsley

200 g (7 oz) silverbeet
  (Swiss chard), stalks
  removed, leaves finely
  chopped
½ quantity Daube (from
  before)
50 g (1¾ oz) cubed bread,
  crusts removed
a pinch of freshly grated
  nutmeg
100 g (3½ oz/1 cup) grated
  parmesan cheese, plus
  extra for topping the
  finished pasta
sea salt and freshly
  ground black pepper

First, make the daube (preferably the day before you eat it). Soak the porcini in warm water for 15 minutes. Discard the water, chop the mushrooms and set aside.

Cut the beef into 1 cm (½ inch) cubes. Splash some of the olive oil into a large saucepan over medium heat, and when it is hot, brown the beef pieces for about 3 minutes, tossing regularly. Remove them from the pan and set aside.

Pour the remaining oil into the pan. Add the butter. When it has melted, add the bone marrow, celery, carrot, onion, garlic and bay leaves. Fry over medium heat for 5 minutes, stirring occasionally with a wooden spoon.

Add the chopped porcini mushrooms and the browned beef and cook, stirring, for 5 minutes. Pour in the wine and let the mixture bubble vigorously for 3 minutes to evaporate the alcohol. Add the chopped tomatoes and about 750 ml (26 fl oz/3 cups) water. Sprinkle in a little salt, grate in a little black pepper, and mix thoroughly.

Now put the lid on the pot and leave to simmer over low heat for 1½ hours.

Drop in the bouquet garni, stir and add a little more water if the mixture seems to be drying out. Cover and simmer for 30 minutes more. Remove the bouquet garni.

Using a slotted spoon, scoop about 300 grams of the meat and mushroom mixture out of the pot and set aside in a large bowl to become the ravioli filling. The remaining meaty liquid will be the sauce.

Here's how to make the ravioli. Start by making the pasta dough. Beat three of the eggs in a large bowl. Make a mound of the flour on a clean work surface, sprinkle on a little salt and make a well in the middle. Slowly pour in the beaten egg mixture and amalgamate it with the flour. Work the mixture until you have a smooth and elastic dough, adding a few drops of warm water if it seems too dry; this should take about 8 minutes.

Form the dough into a ball and let it rest, covered, for 10 minutes.

Sprinkle more flour on your work surface, put the dough on it and knead it for another 10 minutes or so, pushing it out into a flat disc, folding it over, and pushing it out again.

Now cover it and leave to rest for a further 1 hour.

While the dough is resting, make the filling. Heat the olive oil in a frying pan, add the garlic and parsley and fry over medium heat for 2 minutes, stirring often. Now add the chopped silverbeet and cook, stirring, for 5 minutes. Set aside.

Add the cubed bread to the bowl containing the 300 grams of meat mixture and mash it all together. Then add the silverbeet mixture and a grating of nutmeg. Stir in the parmesan, season with a little salt and pepper, and mash the mixture with a fork.

Divide the pasta dough into two evenly sized balls. Roll them out on a floured board so they make two very thin sheets (or put the dough through a pasta machine several times). Use lots of flour on the rolling pin and the board to make sure the pasta sheets don't stick.

Beat the remaining egg. Place one pasta sheet on a flat wide surface, then brush the edges with the beaten egg. Using a teaspoon, dot it with small mounds of filling, in neat rows, with the blobs about 3 cm (1 inch) apart, with no blobs closer than 2 cm (1 inch) to the edge of the sheet.

Gently place the second sheet of dough over the top, and press with your fingers around each filling mound, taking care not to leave air bubbles inside.

If you have a pasta cutter, run it along the rows, vertically and horizontally, and finish each raviolo by crimping the edges with a fork. Or if you prefer a circular shape, upend a small glass over each mound and use the rim to cut out the pasta parcel, then crimp the edges together. Set the ravioli aside to rest for at least 30 minutes.

When you are ready to serve, put the remaining beef daube sauce on to warm (still with chunks of meat in it), and bring a big pot of water to boil. Gently drop the ravioli into the boiling water and boil for 5 minutes.

Put a little of the meat sauce in the bottom of a large serving bowl. Scoop out the ravioli with a slotted spoon and place them in the bowl. Pour the rest of the sauce over them, sprinkle with a little extra grated parmesan and put the bowl in the middle of the table, with a large spoon, so your guests can help themselves.

Barbajuan / Gattafin

(Fried ravioli with silverbeet or pumpkin stuffing)

Barbajuan (literally 'Uncle John') are a kind of fried ravioli which are alleged to be the national dish of Monaco (compulsory eating on 19 November, Monaco's national day), but which are also found in villages south of Genoa under the name gattafin (after the town of Qalta). The filling varies with the seasons, but most often involves the favourite green of this part of the Mediterranean: silverbeet (Swiss chard). The peak time of year for silverbeet is mid-summer, so in winter you might prefer to stuff your Uncle Johns with pumpkin and leek. We give both recipes.

1 egg yolk
a pinch of freshly grated
  nutmeg
60 g (2¼ oz/⅔ cup) grated
  parmesan cheese
100 g (3½ oz) dry ricotta
  cheese
sea salt and freshly
  ground black pepper
1 teaspoon olive oil
a handful of marjoram
  leaves, picked and
  chopped
vegetable oil, for deep-
  frying (optional)

For the pasta
300 g (10½ oz/2 cups)
  plain (all-purpose)
  flour
a pinch of sea salt
1½ tablespoons
  olive oil
100 ml (3½ fl oz) water
1 egg yolk

For the pumpkin filling
½ butternut pumpkin,
  skin removed, flesh
  chopped into large
  chunks

1 leek, pale part only,
  finely chopped
1 tablespoon olive oil

For the silverbeet filling
500 g (1 lb 2 oz) silverbeet
  (Swiss chard) leaves
  (no stalks), chopped
½ head of red radicchio,
  finely chopped
1 bunch flat-leaf (Italian)
  parsley, leaves picked
  and chopped

To make the pasta, place the flour in a mound on a clean, flat work surface and make a well in the middle. Sprinkle in the salt, olive oil and water, and work the flour with your hands until it's a smooth dough (about 10 minutes). Cover and let it rest for 1 hour.

If using the pumpkin filling, bake the pumpkin pieces on an oiled baking tray in a preheated 200°C (400°F) oven for 1 hour. Fry the chopped leek in the olive oil for about 5 minutes, until translucent. Mash the pumpkin and mix it with the leek and a little salt.

If using the silverbeet filling, wilt the silverbeet, radicchio and parsley in a covered saucepan over medium heat with a tiny splash of water for 5 minutes. Dry the mixture with paper towel and finely chop it.

Put the egg yolk in a bowl, grate in a little nutmeg and stir in the parmesan and ricotta. Stir in the pumpkin mixture, or the silverbeet mixture. Sprinkle in a little salt and pepper, the olive oil and marjoram, and mix thoroughly.

Now roll out the dough into a large thin sheet, then cut the sheet into squares about 12 cm (4½ inches) across. Use a tablespoon to place a dollop of mixture on each sheet, slightly towards one side. Fold the dough over the filling and press with your fingers all around to seal the parcel.

To deep-fry the ravioli parcels, pour the vegetable oil into a saucepan, to a depth of about 4 cm (1½ inches), and place over high heat. Fry the ravioli parcels for about 3 minutes on each side, until golden brown. Drain briefly on paper towel and serve hot.

Alternatively, you can bake them on an oiled baking tray at 220°C (425°F) for about 20 minutes, until golden.

GENOA (LIGURIA): Many of the local *salumerias* specialise in focaccia, baked fresh every morning.

Chapter Six

PANE E PIZZE / PAINS ET FOUGASSES /
PA I COQUES

Bread & Pizza

CAMOGLI (LIGURIA):
The town is a treasure
trove of *trompe l'oeil*
facades, where, from a
distance, it's impossible
to tell which balconies,
pediments, shutters and
doorways are real.

Flour, water, heat

When you start to think about it, the creation of bread about 10,000 years ago was an extraordinary feat of the human imagination.

First somebody had to conceive the idea of stripping the seeds off wild grasses, grinding them into a paste, and baking the paste in a fire. Then someone had to figure out how to catch and hold the wild yeasts that can make the dough light and airy; and then how to control the yeast so that a little could produce perfect pizza bases, and a lot could fluff the finest focaccia.

And then they had to realise the importance of patience in the recipe, learning how long to wait so the dough could rise to its potential.

This time we won't try to tell you the Greeks were the ones who started it all (though they *were* big bread consumers). Breadmaking seems to have been perfected in the Middle East centuries before the Greeks started floating around the Med.

But we *are* going to declare that the Romans built their empire on bread in the same way the Greeks fuelled their empire on olive oil. In the 1st century, the Roman satirist Juvenal wrote that all an emperor needed to do, to retain political power, was ensure the populace had plenty of *panem et circenses* (bread and circuses).

Roman politicians had started the practice of handing out free wheat and bread in 123 BC. The first bakers' guild was formed in 168 BC, and by Juvenal's time there were 300 specialist breadmakers serving a city population of about a million.

The security of the grain supply motivated most of Rome's movements through hotter countries. They needed land to grow wheat, so they forcibly enrolled the locals as farmers. They needed to water it, so they built aqueducts. They needed to ship it back home, so they built ports, and roads from those ports.

They needed to convert it to flour, so they built mills and staffed them with slaves. They built ovens at the end of every city block. And they needed markets in which to sell it. Remnants of all of those can be found throughout Catalunya, Provence and Liguria.

Roman Liguria's preferred pastry was focaccia (often flavoured with wine and rosemary), and the taste for that spread round the corner to Nice, where the locals piled on slow-cooked onion and anchovies to make *pissaladière* (which has nothing to do with pizza; see page 177).

Ligurians didn't confine themselves to wheat in their oven-fillers. They ground up chickpeas and mixed the flour with oil and water to make *farinata* (called *socca* in Nice). Genoa is full of *focaccerias* where you can buy slices of *socca* sandwiched within focaccia, along with focaccia stuffed with cheese. This chapter reveals how you can make your own.

Focaccia / Fougasse

(Focaccia with onion and rosemary)

The word *focaccia* and the word *fougasse* come from the Latin word *focus*, which meant hearth or fireplace — the centre of all cooking in European homes until the invention of the stove in the 15th century. It was the first form of bread in the Roman empire, and it was the raw material for the round pizza bases found fossilised in the lava of Pompeii.

Like bread, focaccia and fougasse contain flour, water and yeast. Unlike bread, they also contain olive oil. The difference between Ligurian focaccia and Provençal fougasse is mostly in the shape (focaccia is flatter), and in the amount of oil (Ligurians use more).

This is the recipe for the preferred form of focaccia in Lucio's part of Liguria. We can use it then for the other recipes in this chapter.

Remember that the most important ingredient is patience.

5 g (⅛ oz) active dried
   yeast
½ teaspoon sugar
350 ml (12 fl oz)
   warm water

500 g (1 lb 2 oz/3⅓ cups)
   strong white flour
½ teaspoon sea salt, plus
   extra for sprinkling
80 ml (2½ fl oz/⅓ cup)
   olive oil

Optional extras
a handful of chopped
   rosemary
1 red onion, finely sliced
a handful of stoned
   black olives

In a large bowl, whisk the yeast and sugar with the warm water, and when the yeast has dissolved, stir in half the flour. This will make a sloppy batter. Let it rest, covered, for 2 hours in a warm place, so the yeast will become active and the volume will increase by about one-third.

Place the remaining flour in a mound on a bench. Sprinkle on the salt, and make a well in the middle. Pour the wet mixture into the well and add about 50 ml (1¾ fl oz) of the olive oil. Knead the dough for about 10 minutes, until it forms a firm but sticky ball that is springy to the touch. Brush the ball with a little oil and leave it, covered, in a warm place for another 1 hour.

Turn the dough ball out onto a flat surface, then roll it out to a thickness of about 2 cm (1 inch). You need to shape it to your baking tin — either into a disc or a rectangle. Ideally the baking tin would be about 30 x 40 cm (12 x 16 inches) if rectangular, or have a diameter of 30 cm (12 inches) if round. Flatten the dough to fill the baking tin, and press down with your fingers all over the surface to make sure the depth is even.

Let the dough rest in the pan, covered, for another 30 minutes.

Preheat the oven to 200°C (400°F).

Press the dough down again. Now is the time for any flavourings you care to add. Sprinkle on a little extra sea salt and a handful of chopped rosemary, and/or thinly sliced onion rings, and/or small black olives, which you push down into the dough. Drizzle on a little olive oil. Bake for 30 minutes, until golden.

Serve warm; the bread will stay fresh for a day, if necessary.

Pissaladiera *(Onion and anchovy pie)*

Please don't call this a pizza. While it resembles the thin Ligurian focaccia, or *pizza bianca*, it was born in the city of Nice (where it is called *pissaladiera*, while elsewhere in France it is called *pissaladière*). It is topped only with onions and anchovies and sometimes olives, but never tomato and never cheese.

It is essentially a focaccia (or *fougasse*) covered with onions and a condiment called *pissalat*, a dialect word that means 'salted fish'. *Pissalat* has such ancient origins, it may relate to the *garum* sauce to which the Romans were addicted. It can also be spread on crostini, or used for flavouring cold meats or fish, or sautéed spring vegetables.

The combination of the saltiness of anchovies and the sweetness of caramelised onions is wonderful, intense and irresistible. Who needs tomatoes or cheese?

1 quantity of Focaccia dough (page 174)
500 g (1 lb 2 oz) white onions
50 ml (1¾ fl oz) olive oil
a handful of small pitted black olives

10 anchovy fillets
freshly ground black pepper

For the pissalat
250 g (9 oz) best-quality anchovy fillets in oil

3 garlic cloves
2 thyme sprigs, leaves picked
1 bay leaf
8 black peppercorns
50 ml (1¾ fl oz) olive oil

First make your dough, using the previous recipe. While the ball of dough is resting, peel and thinly slice the onions, then put them in a heavy-based saucepan with the olive oil. Cook them, covered, over low heat for 1 hour, so they become like a soft jam.

While the onions are cooking, make the *pissalat*. Place all the ingredients except the olive oil in a mortar and pound until you obtain a paste. Transfer the paste to a bowl and add the olive oil, mixing with a wooden spoon, so you obtain a thick, smooth consistency.

When the onions are cooked, stir the pissalat into them.

Preheat the oven to 200°C (400°F).

Shape the dough into your baking tin, let it rest for 30 minutes, then spread the onion mixture over the top. Stud the topping with olives and lay the anchovy fillets over in a pattern that pleases you. Grate on some black pepper.

Bake for 30 minutes, or until the onions have started to brown.

Slice and serve warm; the bread will be just as good the next day.

Focaccia con il formaggio
(Cheese focaccia)

In recent years, certain commercial pizza companies have come up with the notion of the 'cheese-stuffed crust'. They'd probably be surprised to learn that it was first described 2200 years ago in a book called *De Re Rustica* ('About Rustic Things') by a Roman writer known as Cato The Elder. He referred to a dish called *scribilita* thus: 'Enclose between sheets of dough slices of cheese.'

This *scribilita* was next mentioned in the records of the Abbey of San Fruttuoso (near Portofino, just east of Genoa) in the year 1189. Apparently a bunch of knights on the way to the crusades were served 'a focaccia of wheat flour and curds and whey'. The document was used as evidence by the Gastronomic Consortium of the town of Recco, just east of Genoa, in 2010, when they were seeking an EU special trademark for the local speciality.

The dish is at its best in a restaurant called Manuelina, and this is our version of their recipe. The cheese they use is stracchino, but you can substitute any creamy soft cheese — ideally Italian, and not brie or camembert, which tend to have ammonia in the skin.

250 g (9 oz/1⅔ cups) plain (all-purpose) flour
sea salt

125 ml (4 fl oz/½ cup) olive oil

350 g (12 oz) soft creamy cheese, ideally stracchino

You will need a shallow metal pizza tray or large paella pan to make this dish.

Place the flour, a pinch of salt and half the olive oil in a bowl and mix well, adding a few drops of water from a wet hand. Place the dough on a clean, flat, lightly floured surface and knead with your hands for about 10 minutes, until you have a smooth soft dough, adding a little water if it seems too dry. Shape into a ball, cover with a cloth and rest in a warm place for 1 hour.

Preheat the oven to 220°C (425°F).

Knead the dough again for about 3 minutes, then split into two even portions. Roll out each ball of dough into a paper-thin circular sheet about the size of your pizza tray or paella pan.

Lightly oil the pan and place one sheet of the dough on it. Break the cheese into small pieces and dot them all over the sheet of dough. Cover with the second sheet of dough, pressing down gently on the edges. Cut off any excess that overlaps the edges.

Sprinkle a little more olive oil over the surface of the dough, spreading it with your hands. Sprinkle on a little salt and tear a few holes in the top to allow the steam to escape. Bake for about 20 minutes, until the focaccia becomes golden.

Cut into wedges and serve warm.

GENOA (LIGURIA):
The lanes around the port are lined with little takeaway shops called *friggitorie* (literally 'fryeries'), selling excellent *farinata* — the chickpea pancake known as *socca* in Nice.

Coca *(Catalan pizza)*

The *coca* (plural *coques*) is the Catalan way of preparing a traditional dish made all around the Mediterranean: crispy flatbread crust with topping, somewhere between a pizza and a focaccia. The word apparently derives from a Latin verb meaning 'to cook'. While the pizza is usually round and the focaccia is usually rectangular, the coca is usually oval-shaped.

There are four main varieties: sweet (with egg and sugar); savoury (with yeast and salt); closed like a calzone; and open, like the *Pissaladiera* (page 177).

The Catalan form of topping is not as thick as in France or Liguria. The simplest form has only pine nuts and oil, but every household elaborates in its own way, adding mushrooms, sliced zucchini (courgette), spinach, olives, anchovies, ham, tomatoes, onions, but rarely cheese. In the version of coca made in Mallorca, an egg yolk and a little sugar are added to the dough, and the topping can include tomatoes. On Saint John's Eve (June 23), the Catalans celebrate with a sweet coca, and include pineapple and glazed cherries in the topping.

This recipe is for a *coca de recapte*, which means 'from the food store', but feel free to improvise.

10 g (¼ oz) active
   dried yeast
250 ml (9 fl oz/1 cup)
   lukewarm water
500 g (1 lb 2 oz/3⅓ cups)
   plain (all-purpose) flour
1 teaspoon sea salt
125 ml (4 fl oz/½ cup)
   olive oil

1 tablespoon dried
   oregano

Suggested toppings
2 red capsicums
   (bell peppers)
2 small eggplants
   (aubergines)
3 red onions, peeled

75 ml (2½ fl oz/⅓ cup)
   olive oil
2 garlic cloves
a handful of flat-leaf
   (Italian) parsley leaves,
   chopped
12 best-quality anchovy
   fillets, in oil

Mix together the yeast and the lukewarm water. Leave for about 5 minutes, to let the yeast froth up and activate.

Place the flour in a large bowl, make a well in the middle and slowly pour the yeasty water into the well. Add the salt and the olive oil and gently mix with your hands until a dough forms. Knead it for about 5 minutes, until the dough no longer sticks to your hands and it is smooth, soft and elastic.

Cover the dough with a damp cloth and let it rest at room temperature for about 1 hour. It should have doubled in size.

If you wish to use our suggested topping, brush the vegetables with some of the olive oil and place them in a lightly oiled baking dish. Bake in a preheated oven at 220°C (425°F) for about 30 minutes, turning them so they cook evenly.

Take the vegetables out of the oven. Turn the oven down to 180°C (350°F).

Peel and seed the capsicums. Peel the eggplants. Take off the blackened outer layer of the onion. Thinly slice all the vegetables, place in a bowl and mix them with the remaining olive oil. Peel the garlic and chop it finely with the parsley. Set aside while you make the *coques*.

Flour your work surface. Divide the dough into six balls, then roll each one into a oval shape about 30 cm (12 inches) long and 1 cm (½ inch) thick.

Place your coca bases on a large greased baking tray and pierce all over with a fork. Splash on a little olive oil and sprinkle a little sea salt.

Bake the coca bases, two at a time, at 180°C (350°F) for 20 minutes. Remove the baking tray from the oven and decorate the *coques* with the roasted vegetable mixture, in rows along the surface. Arrange the anchovies on top, sprinkle with the garlic and parsley mixture, then the dried oregano. Return the tray to the oven and bake for another 10 minutes, until the coca bases are crisp. Serve hot.

Variation: Our friend Janni Kyritsis, whom we inveigled into this project because he is an ancient Greek, created what he calls a 'Greek salad coca'. He covers the semi-baked coca base with halved cherry tomatoes, sliced red onion, pitted Kalamata olives, sliced green capsicum (bell pepper), dried oregano and cubes of feta cheese, and bakes it for another 10 minutes. He serves it with a salad of sliced cucumbers, mint and garlic, dressed with a splash of olive oil and vinegar. We like to imagine the Greek mariners eating it in Empúries 2500 years ago — minus the tomatoes and peppers, of course.

Pizza all'Andrea

(Tomato, garlic and anchovy pizza)

GENOA
Serves 4

East of Genoa, this pastry used to be known as *sardenaira*, because it originally contained sardines, but it's more familiar these days by the name *pizza all'Andrea* — supposedly in honour of a 16th-century Genoese admiral named Andrea Doria, but really, we suspect, because the name sounds like the Niçoise dish *pissaladiera*. It's more of a pizza than a focaccia, because it involves tomatoes.

Treat this as a variation of *Pissaladiera* (page 177), but instead of rolling out the dough so it's 2 cm (¾ inch) thick and fitting it into a deep-sided rectangular pan, roll it out into a disc 5 mm (¼ inch) thick and place on an oiled pizza pan.

Instead of 500 g (1 lb 2 oz) onions, use 250 g (9 oz) onions; when they have cooked for 30 minutes, stir in 50 g (9 oz) finely chopped peeled tomatoes and cook for a further 30 minutes.

Spread that red jam over the dough, top with anchovies, olives and sliced garlic cloves, and bake in a preheated 200°C (400°F) oven for 30 minutes.

COCA
Recipe page 182

PIZZA ALL'ANDREA
Recipe page 183

Nice work and how to get it

It calls itself a flower market, but when you enter Cours Saleya in Nice, it's not the smell of fresh flowers that pulls you towards the eastern end. The fragrance that's filling your nose comes from a stall that's been selling *socca* here since the 1920s.

Socca is a chickpea pancake baked in a wood-fired oven several blocks away and carried, still warm in its giant tray, to the flower market by a bicyclist pulling a little trailer. A lady who asks to be called Theresa (in honour of the original stallholder) slices the *socca* and wraps a few wedges in a cone of greaseproof paper, so customers can munch as they stroll through the market.

We must say Theresa's *socca* is decent comfort food, but not the best interpretation of the dish to be found in Nice. For that you must go around the headland from the old town and find an establishment called Chez Pipo, in Rue Bavastro. You'll know it by the sign outside, which says '*Aqui, si mangia la socca*'.

Hang on a minute. That's not French, that's some kind of Italian, and it seems to say 'Here one eats the socca'. Actually it's not Italian either. It is Niçois dialect. In the men's toilet, there's a poem in local dialect headed 'La Plus Buona Socca De Nissa', which includes this verse: '*La socca ben daurada, En lu plateu redound, Croustilhanta, pebrada, Va toui lu pastissoun.*' Our best attempt at a translation is: 'Socca beautifully golden, in its circular dish, crisp, peppery, is better than all the pastries.'

It's ironic that Nice dialect should be so similar to Italian (the local anthem is called *Nissa La Bella*, for example), considering the city has spent millennia fending off its Ligurian neighbours.

Like the running shoe, the area was named after Nike, the Greek goddess whose name we translate as 'Victory', when the citizens of Massilia (now Marseille) defeated the Liguri tribe there in 350 BC. In 1860, the Niçois voted in a referendum not to become part of Italy, despite the urgings of Giuseppe Garibaldi, who was born there. Garibaldi said: 'To deny the Italianness of Nice is like denying the light of the sun,' but his fellow Niçois preferred to stay French.

In the old town, a terrific bistro called Lu Fran Calin reveals on its menu that it belongs to a society that encourages 'allegiance to the patrimony' of Cuisine Nissarde. The *plats typiques de la région*, described in a kind of Frenchified Italian, include *les lasagnes au four à l'ancienne*; *le tian de courgette*; *les pènne sauce tomate-basilic*; *les raviolis Niçois*; and *les aubergines à la parmigiana*.

The menu declares: 'The art of life, sensuality and authenticity are the first qualities spontaneously attributed to Nice.' To that list of qualities Garibaldi would want to add: 'And a heaping helping of Italian inspiration.'

NICE (PROVENCE): In the flower market, a lady called Theresa started serving *socca* (chickpea pancake) in 1925, and since then every woman who has worked in her stall has adopted the name.

NICE (PROVENCE):
The definitive *socca* is
baked in the wood-fire
oven of Chez Pipo.

Socca / Farinata *(Chickpea pancake)*

One of the masterpieces of Ligurian cooking, the pancake called *farinata*, is made with just a few simple ingredients: chickpea flour, oil and water. It's such a popular comfort food that it spread around the coast to Provence, where it is known as *socca*, a word that seems to derive from the Catalan word *soccarar* (to singe or scorch) — even though the Catalans rarely make it. In Nice, they are so fond of it they consume it for breakfast, morning tea, afternoon tea and a walking-around street snack.

In Liguria it is made in very hot wood-fired ovens on giant copper trays. They are not suitable for home ovens, but you can use any round baking tray made of stainless steel or aluminium, or even a standard oven dish.

The result should be very thin, with a crispy golden crust and a moist interior. The beautiful characteristic of the *farinata*, apart from the taste, is the aroma that you smell at the market in the morning, mingling with the smells of fresh fruit and vegetables.

As a rule, the amount of water has to be three times the amount of flour. If you're wondering why the resting time has to be so long, it is because this will give the *farinata* or *socca* a smoother texture and richer flavour.

300 g (10½ oz/2½ cups) chickpea flour	*125 ml (4 fl oz/½ cup) olive oil*	*sea salt and freshly ground black pepper*

Pour 900 ml (30 fl oz) water into a large bowl. Add the flour, a little at a time, whisking as you pour it in, to prevent lumps forming. If you have lumps you can't eliminate, pass the mixture through a sieve — the end result should be like heavy cream.

Cover the bowl with plastic wrap and let the batter rest for at least 2 hours.

Preheat the oven to its maximum temperature — at least 220°C (425°F).

After 2 hours, skim off any foam on the surface of the batter. Add 2–3 pinches of sea salt (to your taste), then add the olive oil and stir until incorporated.

Lightly oil the base of a baking tray and pour the batter into it, to a depth of not more than 1 cm (½ inch). Any batter left over can be stored in the fridge for up to 2 weeks.

Bake for 25 minutes, until the *farinata* is firm and golden brown.

Take it out of the oven, sprinkle with freshly ground pepper, slice into wedges and serve while it is hot.

Panisse *(Chickpea polenta)*

Panisse is like polenta or porridge, except that it uses chickpea flour instead of corn or oats. Historically it was a favourite of the farmers who carried it into the fields as a snack, to accompany other portable foods.

It was a dish to be served over two days — first to enjoy with olive oil and lemon juice, and second to be thinly sliced and fried in oil and onions.

Today it has been rediscovered and the fashion is to enjoy it as street food, or as part of *aperitivo*. The word *panisse* was adopted for a character in the films of French director Marcel Pagnol, then borrowed by the Californian chef Alice Waters when she named her San Francisco restaurant Chez Panisse.

1 litre (35 fl oz/4 cups) lukewarm water
300 g (10½ oz/2½ cups) chickpea flour

2 tablespoons olive oil, plus extra for dressing
sea salt and freshly ground black pepper

juice of 2 lemons
vegetable oil, for frying

Place the chickpea flour in a large saucepan, then slowly pour in the lukewarm water, a little at a time, whisking as you go. Stir in 2 tablespoons olive oil and whisk until all lumps are eliminated. Let the mixture rest for 3 minutes.

Pour the batter into a large saucepan over low heat and cook gently for 1 hour, stirring regularly with a wooden spoon. The mixture is cooked when it won't stick to the sides of the saucepan.

You can now serve it hot, dressed with olive oil, lemon juice and pepper.

Or you can spread the mixture evenly over a cold surface and let it cool. When it has set, cut it into strips about 2 cm (½ inch) wide and 8 cm (3 inches) long. Fry the strips in about 4–5 cm (2 inches) of hot vegetable oil over high heat, until they are golden; this will take about 3 minutes. Dry them on kitchen paper, sprinkle them with sea salt and a bit of lemon juice and serve them hot. Or, use them to dip into the four different coloured sauces on pages 50–51.

Chapter Seven
ZUPPE / POTAGES / SOPES
Soups & Stews

Membre fondateur de la
Charte de la Bouillabaisse

HUILE D'OLIVE

MARSEILLE (PROVENCE):
On its wall, Le Rhul restaurant
boasts of being a founding member
of the society that protects the
integrity of *bouillabaisse.*

Blame it on the Greeks

This is a chapter about what Ligurians would call zuppe *(the plural of* zuppa*). The word should not be translated merely as 'soup'.*

A *zuppa* is thicker and more crammed with bits than anything an English speaker would picture as a soup. When used in *zuppa di pesce*, it means a seafood stew. When used in *zuppa inglese*, it means bits of sponge with custard and jelly.

Zuppa was the second recipe invented by humans — the first being 'throw animal onto fire and burn until edible'. The breakthrough was the invention of the pot — initially a hollowed-out stone that could hold water, until some genius realised that powdered stone could be moulded into a bowl shape and baked in the fire, next to the dinner animal.

Once they had pots, humans could start adding leaves and grasses to improve the flavour of the chopped-up creatures and vegetables that were stewing in the water.

Terracotta pots and bowls were traded by the Greeks in the *emporions* they set up around the Mediterranean, so it's reasonable to argue that zuppa was what brought civilisation to the tribes of Europe. Pots — particularly the Greek three-legged *kakavi* — enabled people to consume and enjoy a far wider range of foodstuffs, and, sitting on the fire to simmer all day, gave people time to reflect on higher things, like religion, politics and art.

That's why Europeans have developed so many labels for their *zuppe* — often named after the containers they are cooked in, which shows due respect to the Greek originators. Ligurians are familiar with seafood 'soups' called *cacciuco, brodetto, ciambotta, burrida* (or *buridda*) and *cioppino* (or *ciuppin*), not to mention inland concoctions such as *minestrone, brodo, brodetto, mesciua* and *vellutata*. Provençals know *bisque, bourride, bouillon, bouillabaisse, potage, consommé, oille, ragout* and *chaudière* (which gave us the word 'chowder'). Catalans know *caldereta, escudella, estofat, ollada, ajoblanco, gazpatxo, platillo* and *salmorejo*.

So this must be the most historical chapter in this book. And the most civilising of the *zuppe* in this chapter were made with seafood, based on the original Greek recipe, plus the tomatoes and peppers that arrived from the Americas 2000 years after the Greeks.

And even the Ligurians and the Catalans would grudgingly concede that the emperor of all *zuppe* is *Bouillabaisse* (page 196), which is technically, of course, both a soup and a stew.

Bouillabaisse *(Fish soup with fish stew)*

A great bouillabaisse is two meals: a dense and intense fish soup (on which are floating little rafts of rouille), and then a pile of seafood which has been poached in that soup. At restaurants in Marseille it's usually served as two courses in a long lunch, but you could serve it over two days if you prefer to eat more lightly.

Here we present the two recipes that bring the bouillabaisse together. We begin with the sieved purée that the French humbly call a *bouillon* and the Ligurians proudly call *ciuppin* (pronounced 'choopeen', dialect for 'little soup').

Rouille (see page 48, version 2), to serve
2 baguettes, thinly sliced and lightly toasted
grated gruyère cheese, to serve

For the bouillon
2.5 kg (5 lb 8 oz) white-fleshed fish, such as leatherjacket, garfish, monkfish and rockfish; ask your fishmonger to scale and fillet them, reserving the bones and heads
½ teaspoon saffron threads
3 garlic cloves, chopped
2 thyme sprigs, leaves picked and finely chopped
olive oil, for drizzling and pan-frying
freshly ground black pepper
1 white onion, finely chopped

1 fennel bulb, finely chopped
1 carrot, finely chopped
1 celery stalk, finely chopped
3 bay leaves
3 large ripe tomatoes, peeled, seeded and chopped
1 tablespoon tomato paste (concentrated purée)
50 ml (1¾ fl oz) white wine

For the fish stew
a few splashes of olive oil
10 medium potatoes, peeled and sliced
2 white onions, thinly sliced
4 garlic cloves, finely chopped
4 tomatoes, peeled, seeded and chopped
1 tablespoon tomato paste (concentrated purée)
2 tablespoons Herbes de Provence (see page 21)

1 bouquet garni, made by tying together sprigs of fresh thyme, rosemary, sage and oregano
1 large cuttlefish, or 3 small cuttlefish, cleaned and chopped
1.5 kg (3 lb 5 oz) whole firm-fleshed white fish, such as snapper, bream, sea bass, hake or john dory, cleaned and scaled
1.5 kg (3 lb 5 oz) whole delicate-fleshed fish, such as whiting, flounder, plaice, haddock or red mullet, cleaned and scaled
15 mussels, scrubbed clean, beards removed
1 teaspoon saffron threads
sea salt and freshly ground black pepper
2 litres (70 fl oz/8 cups) Bouillon (from above)

Start by making the *bouillon*. Wash the heads and bones of the fish to remove all the blood, then chop them into small pieces and set aside. Chop the fish fillets into chunks and mix them in a bowl with the saffron, garlic, thyme, a few splashes of olive oil and a few grinds of black pepper. Let the mixture marinate for 15 minutes.

Splash about another 3 tablespoons olive oil into a heavy-based, high-sided saucepan, place it over low heat and add the onion, fennel, carrot, celery and bay leaves. Fry gently for about 8 minutes. Turn the heat up to medium, then add the reserved fish bones and heads and fry for 5 minutes. Now add the chopped fish fillets (with their marinade) and fry for 3 minutes more. Stir in the tomatoes and tomato paste and fry for a further 2 minutes. Pour in the wine and let it boil for 3 minutes to evaporate the alcohol.

Pour in about 2 litres (70 fl oz/8 cups) water, or enough to cover the mixture. Bring back to the boil, then leave to simmer for 1 hour. Skim off any scum that forms on the top.

Remove the bay leaves. Purée the remaining ingredients using a food processor (or grind them slowly through a mouli), then push the purée through a strainer to eliminate any remaining bones. You now have a bouillon in which you can poach other fish for a bouillabaisse, or serve as a soup in which you can float toasts rubbed with garlic and topped with rouille and a sprinkling of grated gruyère cheese.

To make the *bouillabaisse*, splash a generous amount of olive oil into a large, heavy-based, high-sided saucepan. Add the potato slices, onion, garlic, tomatoes, tomato paste, Herbes de Provence, bouquet garni and the cuttlefish. Mix them all up with your hands, making sure the potatoes are thoroughly coated with the tomatoes and oil, and have a uniform colour.

Place the pan over medium heat. After 2 minutes, stir and add the firm-fleshed whole fish on top. Pour in the bouillon; the fish should be completely covered in liquid, so top up with water if it's not. Bring to the boil, then cook over medium heat for 5 minutes. Now add the delicate-fleshed fish and the mussels.

Toast the saffron (the best way is wrap the bundle of threads in foil and toss the small parcel in a dry frying pan over high heat for 1 minute). Sprinkle the toasted saffron over the fish, along with a little salt and pepper. Shake the pan to settle the ingredients, then bring the mixture back to the boil. Lower the heat and simmer for 20 minutes.

Using a slotted spoon, gently take the seafood out of the soup, without breaking up the fish. Arrange the fish, the potatoes, and the mussels on a large serving platter. Discard the bouquet garni.

Splash a few spoonfuls of the soup over the seafood to keep it all moist. Spread the rouille on small ovals of toast. Ladle the soup into eight bowls and float two or three rouille rafts on top of each bowl.

Give your guests large plates and plenty of spoons and forks so they can serve themselves the fish, the potatoes, and the mussels. Leave a bowl of rouille and a bowl of grated gruyère on the table, and plenty more toasts for dipping.

BOUILLABAISSE
Recipe page 196

The Greeks brought their recipe for a fish stew called 'kakavia' to Marseille in 600 BC, and used saffron to give it a kick. The recipe was augmented with tomatoes and potatoes 2000 years later.

The rules of la bouille

In Marseille, walk up Rue Canebiére (Cannabis Street) from the spot where the Greeks stepped ashore 2600 years ago, and turn right into Rue Longue des Capucins ('Long Street of the Capuchin monks'). At number 10, step inside a shop called Saladin Epices Du Monde, pass the giant bowls of multicoloured olives and the boxes of dried mushrooms, and look at the legacy of those Greeks: 80 hessian bags set out on long tables, containing dried flavourings for all the great dishes of the Mediterranean.

The labels on the bags include *Épices paella*; *Preparation pesto*; *Mélange pour mozzarella alla Caprese*; *Court bouillon poisson*; *Nyora Espagnol concasse*; *Mélange poisson grillade*; *Sel de Camargue*; and *Preparation bruschetta à la tomate*.

The only significant absence is any bag labelled as being helpful in the preparation of *bouillabaisse*. No shopkeeper would have the nerve to offer that kind of shortcut in Marseille. *Bouillabaisse* (page 196) is part of this city's identity, and there are strict rules about getting it right. To study them, you must take a ten-minute taxi ride from where the Greeks landed (now called Le Vieux Port) to a blue and white clifftop restaurant called Le Rhul. Since 1948, Le Rhul has been serving a definitive bouillabaisse (in two courses, of course).

We say definitive, because Le Rhul was a founding member of the Bouillabaisse Charter, a club (cabal? conspiracy?) of nine restaurateurs who set the rules. The name, you need to know, is an amalgam of two Provençal verbs: *bouillir* (to boil), and *abaisser* (to lower heat). The charter begins: *La Bouillabaisse, plat Marseillais par excellence, comporte des ingrédients bien précis qu'il importe d'utiliser, si l'on veut respecter la tradition et ne pas tromper le client.* ('The bouillabaisse, superb Marseille dish, consists of very precise ingredients which it is important to use, if one wishes to respect the tradition and not trick the customer.')

Apart from the tomatoes, potatoes and pimento, the fish stew defined in the charter would be totally familiar to the Greeks who defeated the local Liguri tribe, built the city of Massilia about 600 BC, and began a trading relationship with the Romans that kept the city from being absorbed into the Roman empire until 49 BC, when it was annexed by Julius Caesar because the Marseillais didn't back him in his war against Pompey. If you want to see what the landscape looked like at the time the Greeks rowed up, catch a bus or train to the neighbouring village of Cassis and board one of the boats that regularly motor through turquoise waters around the extraordinary limestone fjords known as Les Calanques.

Then head for Le Grand Bleu restaurant in Cassis to eat an excellent rendition of whatever was their catch of the day. Yes, they'll make you a bouillabaisse if you insist. But you're out of Marseille now, and the rules no longer apply, so be careful.

MARSEILLE (PROVENCE):
From Le Rhul restaurant, diners can look up from their *bouillabaisse* and see the Château d'If, the island fortress where the Man in the Iron Mask was allegedly imprisoned.

MARSEILLE (PROVENCE):
The boats moored in the
Le Vieux Port 2600 years
ago would have been
Greek galleys.

Bourride *(White fish soup with orange aïoli)*

The word 'soup' does not do justice to bourride (also known as *borrida* and *bourrido* in the Occitan dialects of Provence), which is a distant white cousin of *Bouillabaisse* (page 196), but just as delicious. As served in the town of Sète (at the end of the Canal du Rhône, which once connected Paris with the Mediterranean), it presents as pieces of white fish covered with a thick white sauce, beautifully flavoured with orange zest and eggy aïoli. The Sètois say it's essential to drink rosé with bourride, since a white wine is too wimpy and a red is too rich.

2 kg (4 lb 8 oz) john dory
   fillets, monkfish or
   other firm white fish
   fillets (bones and heads
   reserved for stock)
3 tablespoons mild-
   flavoured olive oil
1 leek, pale part only,
   finely chopped
1 white onion,
   chopped

1 carrot, roughly chopped
1 fennel heart, roughly
   chopped
zest from 1 small orange
320 ml (11 fl oz) dry white
   wine
2 litres (70 fl oz/8 cups)
   fish stock (see page 22)
600 g (1 lb 5 oz) potatoes,
   peeled and sliced into
   discs

2 pinches of saffron
   threads
1 bowl of Aïoli (page 53)
2 baguettes, thinly sliced
   and lightly toasted
1 garlic clove, cut in half
   (to rub on the toasts)
Rouille (page 48), to serve
   (optional)

Cut the fish fillets into large pieces and set aside.

Heat the olive oil in a high-sided saucepan over medium heat, then add the leek, onion, carrot, fennel and orange zest. Fry for about 10 minutes, stirring regularly.

Turn up the heat and stir in the wine, the stock, the potatoes and the saffron. Boil for a further 12 minutes. Turn down the heat, add the fish pieces and simmer for 12 minutes.

Using a slotted spoon, gently remove the fish and set the pieces aside.

Take the pan off the heat and add the aïoli to the soup. Stir with a wooden spoon. Place the pan back over a low heat and stir for about 3 minutes, until the mixture is smooth and creamy. Do not let the soup boil.

Ladle the soup into individual bowls. Top with the fish pieces and serve with slices of baguette that have been toasted and rubbed with a cut garlic clove.

To add a little colour, you could accompany this with a bowl of *rouille*.

Romescada / Sarsuela / Suquet de peix

(Three Catalan fish soups)

These three classic Catalan soups have enough similarities to let us group their recipes together, though we may risk offending some micro-regionalists. We're making the bold assumption that *sarsuela* is like a *romescada* with almonds, and *suquet* is like a *romescada* with potatoes.

Romescada gets its name from the supposed origin of the dish in the town of Tarragona (founded by the Romans about 200 BC). But it's unlikely to taste much like any fish stew the Romans ate, since the key ingredient of the romesco sauce is the hot nyora pepper, which didn't reach Spain (from the Americas) until the 16th century. Because nyora peppers are hard to find outside Spain, we've substituted a mix of capsicums (bell peppers) and standard chilli.

We first read about *sarsuela* in a book by Pablo Picasso about his favourite Catalan foods, and when we learned that it was also a favourite of Salvador Dali, we had to try it. *Sarsuela* is the Catalan spelling of the Spanish zarzuela, which seems to derive from the word *zarza*, meaning bramble or nettle. But brambles are not an ingredient of this stew. *Zarzuela* is a type of operatic dance-drama popular in Madrid since the 17th century. These operas were first performed in a royal hunting lodge called the Palacio de la Zarzuela ('Palace of the Bramble'), and presumably the guests of King Philip IV enjoyed a fishy treat before or during their musical entertainment.

The word *suquet* just means 'little juice'. The Latin root word entered English as 'succulent', and this soup certainly is. Because it includes potatoes, *suquet* is also the most stew-like of the three treats.

300 g (10½ oz) clams (vongole)
1 glass white wine
2 litres (70 fl oz/8 cups) fish stock (see page 22)
2 tablespoons olive oil
600 g (1 lb 5 oz) john dory, or other white-fleshed fish fillets, cut into pieces

600 g (1 lb 5 oz) rockfish, perch or redfish fillets, cut into pieces
600 g (1 lb 5 oz) scampi or crayfish
a bowl of Romesco sauce (page 44), to serve
sea salt
crusty bread, to serve

For the sofregit
60 ml (2 fl oz/¼ cup) olive oil
1 onion, thinly sliced
2 garlic cloves, chopped
1 large green chilli, seeded and chopped
200 g (7 oz) ripe red tomatoes, peeled, seeded and chopped

Put the clams in a saucepan. Pour in the wine, cover and place over high heat. Cook for about 5 minutes, until the shells open, and take the pan off the heat.

Now make the *sofregit*. Pour the olive oil into a deep-sided saucepan over medium heat. Add the onion and fry, stirring often, for about 8 minutes. Add the garlic and the chilli and fry for 2 minutes more, stirring regularly. Add the tomatoes, mix thoroughly, turn the heat down to low and simmer for 15 minutes, stirring regularly.

Add the fish stock to the *sofregit*, along with the cooking liquid from the clams. Simmer for another 10 minutes.

Meanwhile, splash the olive oil into a non-stick frying pan over medium heat. In batches, sear the fish fillets and the scampi for 2 minutes on each side. Set aside.

Stir 2 tablespoons of romesco sauce into the simmering stock mixture. After a minute, add the scampi and the seared fish fillets. After one minute more add the clams in their shells.

Simmer for 5 minutes more over medium heat. Season with salt if needed, then serve with crusty bread for dipping, with more romesco in a bowl on the side.

Variations: To make this into a *sarsuela*, you can include strips of calamari and chopped jamón or prosciutto, which should be fried with the onion from the beginning of the *sofregit*. Instead of the romesco sauce, add 100 g (3½ oz) blanched almonds, which you have crushed in a mortar. Some versions include ½ teaspoon ground cinnamon and 3 tablespoons dry sherry, which are added when you stir the stock into the *sofregit*. And one spectacular version involves pouring flaming rum over the mixture when it arrives on the table (as with a Christmas pudding) and waiting until the flames die out before serving.

To make this into a *suquet de peix*, add 500 g (1 lb 2 oz) peeled, chopped potatoes to the pot immediately after adding the stock, and, instead of the romesco, stir in 2 tablespoons *Picada* (page 60), along with 2 pinches of saffron threads — making it a little more like something the Greeks might have eaten.

ROMESCADA
Recipe page 206

ESCUDELLA
Recipe page 210

Escudella i carn d'olla

(Chicken and pig's trotter stew, with pasta and meatballs)

This is a traditional slow-cooked casserole, ideal for mid-winter, and in Europe is often served as two courses on Christmas Day. It was first described in a Spanish cookbook published in the 14th century. The ingredients can vary seasonally, but should include vegetables, legumes and several types of meat — most importantly a pig's trotter, which contributes a comforting gelatinous texture.

Escudella means 'bowl', and as usual, every Catalan family has a different recipe. Some even stuff the pasta shells with minced (ground) meat. Our version contains large meatballs, called *pilota*.

This dish does take a considerable time to make, but the shared experience is worth it.

1 pig's trotter, cut in half by your butcher

300 g (10½ oz) stewing beef, on the bone (shank or osso bucco is ideal)

2 chicken marylands (leg quarters)

1 black sausage, or 1 Italian fennel sausage (casing removed)

200 g (7 oz) bacon

2 tablespoons olive oil

1 white onion, thinly sliced

5 garlic cloves, thinly sliced

1 cabbage, quartered and sliced

4 carrots, diced

1 turnip, diced

2 celery stalks

400 g (14 oz/2 cups) dried chickpeas, soaked in water overnight

sea salt and freshly ground black pepper

300 g (10½ oz) conchiglioni pasta (shell-shaped)

best-quality olive oil, for drizzling

For the 'pilota' (meatballs)

2 slices white bread, crusts removed

milk, for soaking the bread

1 egg

2 garlic cloves, finely chopped

2 tablespoons finely chopped flat-leaf (Italian) parsley

sea salt and freshly ground black pepper

250 g (9 oz) minced (ground) beef

250 g (9 oz) minced (ground) pork

1 tablespoon pine nuts

3 oregano sprigs, leaves picked and roughly chopped

plain (all-purpose) flour, for dusting

To make the meatballs, soak the bread in enough milk to cover for a few minutes. Gently squeeze out the excess moisture and set aside. Break the egg into a large bowl, add the garlic and parsley, season with salt and pepper and beat together. Add the beef and pork and mix thoroughly. Add the pine nuts, oregano and bread, mixing well to combine all the ingredients. Using your hands, mould the mixture into spheres about the size of golf balls. Dust them in flour and set aside.

Rinse the pig's trotter, the beef and the chicken very well, then put all the meats in a large stockpot. Cover with about 4 litres (140 fl oz/16 cups) cold water and bring to the boil. Reduce the heat and simmer gently for about 30 minutes, skimming the top regularly.

In the meantime, heat the olive oil in a frying pan over medium heat with the onion and garlic and sauté gently for 8 minutes. Add this mixture to the stockpot, along with the cabbage, carrots, turnip and celery.

Drain the soaked chickpeas and add them to the pot. Season with salt and pepper, mix well and simmer for a further 2 hours. If the mixture appears to be drying out, you can stir in a little hot water.

Now add the meatballs and simmer for a further 20 minutes. At this point, the chickpeas should be soft, and the meat falling off the bone. Using a large slotted spoon, remove the meats and vegetables from the soup. Scrape off any meat and marrow remaining on the bones, keeping the meat and marrow and discarding the bones.

Pour three-quarters of the broth through a sieve into a bowl and allow to cool, so you can skim the fat from the surface. Return the meats and vegetables to the stockpot off the heat, so they can rest and remain moist.

Place the drained broth into a large saucepan and bring it to the boil, then stir in the pasta shells and cook according to the recommended time on the packet. Serve the pasta soup as an appetiser.

For the second course, place all the meats and vegetables in a large serving dish, top it with some of the reserved broth, and place it in the middle of the table for your guests to help themselves. Have some good olive oil and sea salt available for final dressing.

You can accompany this stew with boiled potatoes dressed in olive oil, and a salad of green beans, tomato and onions scented with finely chopped basil.

Caldereta de llagosta *(Lobster soup)*

This special-occasion dish, served in some of Barcelona's finest restaurants, originated on the island of Minorca, which is proud of its Catalan heritage and just as proud of its spiny lobsters. Usually a *caldereta* (named for the terracotta pot in which it is cooked) is made with beef, but the Minorcans adapted it to their catch of the day. If you can't find very fresh lobsters, feel free to replace that ingredient with fillets of your favourite fish.

The Minorcans believe *caldereta* tastes best if it has been allowed to rest for at least 5 hours, before being served lukewarm.

5 tablespoons olive oil
3 white onions, finely chopped
3 garlic cloves, chopped
1 large green chilli, seeded and finely sliced
5 tomatoes, peeled, seeded and sliced
2 lobsters, weighing about 1 kg (2 lb 4 oz) each

100 ml (3½ fl oz) white wine
1 litre (35 fl oz/4 cups) fish stock (see page 22)
2 slices ciabatta bread, fried in a little oil
60 g (2¼ oz) almonds, toasted
3 flat-leaf (Italian) parsley sprigs, leaves picked and chopped

2 baguettes, thinly sliced and lightly toasted
sea salt and freshly ground black pepper

Splash the olive oil into a large, deep-sided saucepan (ideally terracotta) and place over medium heat. Add the onion and fry for 5 minutes. Add half the garlic and all the chilli and fry for 3 minutes more. Add the tomatoes and simmer for another 10 minutes. This is your *sofregit*.

While your *sofregit* is simmering, cut the heads off the lobsters and remove the tail meat from the shells. Cut the tails into medallions and set them aside.

Cut the lobster heads in half. Scoop out and reserve the material inside the heads (the coral). Cut the heads in half again and add the shells to the simmering *sofregit*. Pour in the wine and let the mixture boil for 3 minutes to evaporate the alcohol. Taste and season with salt and pepper. Add the stock, shake the pan, turn down the heat and let it simmer for about 5 minutes.

In the meantime, place the remaining garlic in a blender, along with the reserved orange coral and interior of the lobster heads. Add the pan-fried bread, toasted almonds, half the parsley and a splash of olive oil. Pulse-blend until you have a smooth paste.

Add the paste and the lobster medallions to the cooking pot and stir gently. Cook over medium heat for 3 minutes. Take the soup off the heat, remove the pieces of shell, and let it rest for 3 minutes.

Sprinkle with the remaining parsley and serve with toasted baguette slices.

AMEGLIA (LIGURIA):
The town looks across to the marble mountains of Carrara and down to the fishing village of Bocca di Magra, where Lucio Galletto's family built their trattoria on the beach in 1950.

Cigrons amb xoriço

(Chickpea and sausage stew)

The Romans loved chickpeas, and planted them wherever they spread their empire. The greatest orator of ancient times, Marcus Tullius Cicero, was named after a chickpea. One myth said this was because his father had a wart the size of a *cicer* on his nose; another said Marcus Tullius used to fill his mouth with *cicers* in order to train himself to speak clearly — but more likely it was because his grandparents had been traders in *cicers*, just as anyone called Fabius had a background in fava beans, and anyone called Lentulus had a background in lentils. Cicero was urged to change his name when he entered politics, but he said his performance would elevate the humble chickpea to noble status.

If you want to celebrate the wisdom of Cicero by eating as he would have done, make this recipe without capsicums and tomatoes.

3 cups dried or tinned
  chickpeas
sea salt and freshly
  ground black pepper
2 bay leaves
2–3 tablespoons
  olive oil
250 g (9 oz) fresh chorizo
  or Italian sausages

1 white onion, finely
  chopped
200 g (7 oz) bacon, diced
1 red capsicum (bell
  pepper), finely chopped
2 garlic cloves, crushed
800 g (1 lb 12 oz) fresh
  ripe tomatoes, peeled,
  seeded and diced

3 thyme sprigs
1 teaspoon hot chilli
  flakes, or 2 finely
  chopped fresh hot
  red chillies

If you're using dried chickpeas, soak them overnight in about 2 litres (70 fl oz/8 cups) cold water with a couple of pinches of salt. Drain them and place into a large soup pot, cover with cold water and place over medium heat. Add the bay leaves and bring to the boil. Reduce the heat to low, cover and simmer gently for an hour. Skim off any foam, season with salt and pepper and simmer for another hour, or until tender. Drain the chickpeas over a bowl, reserving 500 ml (17 fl oz/2 cups) of the cooking liquid.

If you're using tinned chickpeas, bring them to a boil with the bay leaves, simmer for 5 minutes, then drain them and reserve 500 ml (17 fl oz/2 cups) of the cooking liquid.

Splash a little olive oil into a large casserole dish and brown the sausages on all sides over medium heat. Remove, slice and set aside. Splash a bit more olive oil into the same pan, still over medium heat, then sauté the onion and the bacon for 8 minutes, or until the onion is soft.

Add the capsicum and continue frying and stirring for another 8 minutes or so, until everything is tender. Now add the garlic and stir for a few minutes. Add the tomatoes, sausage slices and thyme. Check the seasoning and add salt and pepper to taste.

Cook over medium heat for 10 minutes, stirring regularly. Now add the chickpeas, chilli and the reserved 500 ml (17 fl oz/2 cups) of chickpea cooking water. Bring to the boil, mixing thoroughly.

Turn the heat down to low and simmer, covered, for about 15 minutes, until the chickpeas are very tender. Taste for seasoning and serve with toasted bread rubbed with garlic.

BARCELONA (CATALUNYA):
All manner of weird Mediterranean
shellfish are on sale at the Sant
Josep *boqueria*.

Chapter Eight

SEMPLICI PIACERI / PLAISIRS SIMPLES /
PLAERS SIMPLES

Simple Pleasures

EMPÚRIES (CATALUNYA):
The scene is almost as
peaceful as when the Greeks
first landed in Spain 2600
years ago, a rare break from
the crush of the Costa Brava.

Old, new, rich, poor

You might consider the title of this chapter, Simple Pleasures, to be ironic, given that the recipes include lobster and quail.

To be frank, this is a collection of leftovers — dishes we thought were important for one reason or another, but which didn't fit into any of the categories we'd set up for earlier chapters. And while some of the dishes in earlier chapters are pretty complex, designed to be shared by up to eight people as fabulous family feasts, the recipes in this chapter are more straightforward, able to be prepared for an intimate dinner for two, even if the ingredients are occasionally extravagant.

We had to recognise the Catalan habit (apparently dating back to the Romans) of mixing the produce of the sea and the produce of the mountains in a series of dishes called *Mar i muntanya* (page 222). We also remembered the wonderful version we consumed at the Hotel Aigua Blava on the Costa Brava, where the elegant white-jacketed head waiter Pepe Rojas and his lovely assistant carefully dissected the chicken and the lobster and lifted them from a silver salver onto our plates, then covered the pieces with a silky sauce.

We included the whole baked fish from Collioure (page 231) because we like to imagine Pablo Picasso with a bib around his neck tucking into it in front of a beaming Pauline Pous.

We had a go at *Homard à la Provençal* (the baked lobster of Nice; page 225) because we wanted to deal with the mythology around a 19th-century dish sometimes called *lobster à l'Amoricaine* and sometimes *lobster à l'Americaine*.

The *Brandacujun* (salt cod with olives and potatoes; page 238) is a specialty of the Riviera di Ponente, to the west of Genoa. It's often on the menu of Il Mulino restaurant in Varazze (near the best basil in the world; see page 34).

The quail and figs recipe (page 243) is an adaption of an old Provençal stew of chicken and figs. We accompanied it with the ancient grain called farro, popular in Liguria for 3000 years, because we hadn't found any other way to include this vital ingredient in this book.

Llenties estofades (lentils and chorizo; page 244) is the kind of dish that would be served by the Agut-Manubens family, cooked by the mother and daughter chefs, at Can Culleretes, the oldest restaurant in Catalunya.

From Le Grand Bleu in Cassis, near Marseille, comes the red mullet and potatoes (page 237). We wish the English language could come up with a more poetic name for the beautiful pink swimmers known to the French as *rouget*, the Italians as *triglia*, and the Greeks as *barbunya*.

From the Gambero Rosso restaurant in the Cinque Terre village of Vernazza comes the *tian* of potatoes and sardines on page 228 — although on their menu they use the local name *tegame*, only slightly evolved from the ancient Greek word for the cooking pots that were traded in every *emporion*.

Mar i muntanya

(Chicken and prawn casserole)

The name means 'sea and mountain'. In English-speaking countries, the idea of 'surf 'n' turf' seems like a kitschy throwback to the 1970s, when restaurants showed off by putting pieces of lobster on fillet steak. For 1000 years, the Catalans have seen nothing funny in the concept of combining the bounty of the sea with the bounty of the land, often as a way of extending ingredients that were in short supply — as long as the elements are cooked together in a way that enhances the flavour of both. *Mar i muntanya* is a specialty of north-eastern Catalunya.

a generous splash of olive oil
8 boneless chicken thighs
3 spring onions (scallions), chopped
2 garlic cloves
4 tomatoes, grated to the skin

60 ml (2 fl oz / ¼ cup) white wine
sea salt and freshly ground black pepper
12 large raw prawns (shrimp)
Picada (page 60), to serve

steamed white rice, to serve
½ teaspoon saffron threads

Heat a generous splash of olive oil in a non-stick heavy-based saucepan. Brown the chicken pieces over medium heat for about 3 minutes each side, until golden brown. Take the chicken out of the pan and set aside.

In the same pan, with the same oil, sizzle the spring onion for 6 minutes, stirring often. Add the garlic and, a minute later, the tomatoes. Mix thoroughly and cook for 5 minutes, until most of the tomato liquid has evaporated and the onion is very soft. Pour in the wine and let it boil for 3 minutes to evaporate the alcohol.

Return the chicken to the pan, season with salt and pepper, and stir in 500 ml (17 fl oz/2 cups) water. Bring to the boil, then reduce the heat to low and simmer, uncovered, for 40 minutes.

Add the whole prawns, stir well and cook for a further 10 minutes. Now stir in about 2 tablespoons of *picada* and cook for another 10 minutes.

Serve in a big bowl in the middle of the table, next to a bowl of steamed white rice through which you have stirred the saffron (which you've steeped in 2 tablespoons of warm water for 5 minutes). Serve the remaining picada in a bowl. Diners can help themselves and put lots of sauce on their rice.

Homard à la Provençal

(Baked lobster)

This dish is sometimes served in restaurants outside Provence under the name *lobster à l'Armoricaine,* or even *lobster à l'Americaine,* but it has nothing to do with Armorica (the old name for Brittany, on the Atlantic coast), or the United States (except that Americans like to eat it). Until the late 19th century it was called just *lobster Provençale,* because of the tomato-based sauce it is baked with — known, mysteriously, as *sauce vierge* (virgin sauce).

If you find lobster too expensive, substitute prawns (shrimp), scampi, or any other large shellfish, and cut the baking time in half.

4 large tomatoes, peeled, seeded and diced
6 basil leaves, finely sliced
80 ml (2½ fl oz/⅓ cup) olive oil
4 garlic cloves, finely chopped

1 large lemon, juiced and finely sliced
sea salt and freshly ground black pepper
4 lobsters, cut in half
125 g (4½ oz) butter, in small pieces

125 ml (4 fl oz/½ cup) white wine
1 sprig each of thyme, rosemary and oregano, leaves picked and chopped

First make the virgin sauce. Place the diced tomatoes in a bowl with the basil, olive oil, half the chopped garlic and the juice of the lemon. Sprinkle on a little salt and pepper. Mix all the ingredients thoroughly and set aside.

Preheat the oven to 200°C (400°F).

Place the eight lobster halves in a flameproof baking dish, cut side up. Spread over them the butter, the remaining garlic, and the virgin sauce, then intersperse them with pieces of lemon. Place in the oven and bake for 12 minutes.

Take the baking dish out of the oven and place it over medium heat on the stovetop. Remove the lemons. Splash in the wine, shake the pan, and let the alcohol evaporate for 3 minutes.

Toss in the fresh herbs and shake the pan again. Serve two lobster halves to each guest, pouring the sauce from the pan over them.

White rice goes well with this dish.

TELLARO (LIGURIA):
This village on the Gulf of
Poets (so named because
Byron and Shelley took
holidays nearby) has
a speciality of ravioli
stuffed with red mullet.

Tian de sardines / Tegame di sardine *(Potato and sardine bake)*

Tian is Niçois and Ligurian dialect for the Italian word *tegame*, a long pan with two handles, deriving from the Greek word *teganon*, which makes us think this must have been one of the cooking implements they brought with them when they crossed the seas with their saffron, their olives and their fish soup recipe.

The *tian* is a kind of savoury layer cake, made with sliced vegetables and sometimes fish. The basic recipe we're suggesting here involves sardines, because we haven't used them earlier in the book, but you can replace them with anchovies.

The two recipes that follow this are also variations on *tian*, but further and further west — one a speciality of Cassis, near Marseille, and the other a speciality of Collioure, near the Spanish border.

4 medium potatoes
1 garlic clove
olive oil, for drizzling
3 tomatoes, peeled, seeded and diced
2 rosemary sprigs, leaves picked and chopped

600 g (1 lb 5 oz) fresh sardines, filleted and opened like a book
1 tablespoon finely chopped flat-leaf (Italian) parsley
1 tablespoon finely chopped fresh oregano

sea salt
2 tablespoons pine nuts
3 tablespoons dry breadcrumbs
80 g (2¾ oz) small black olives

Preheat the oven to 180°C (350°F). Peel the potatoes, wash them and slice them thinly. Cut the garlic clove in half and lavishly rub the cut sides over the surface of a high-sided baking dish. Splash in some olive oil and tilt the dish to spread it around.

Spread half the tomatoes over the base of the dish. Sprinkle with about one-third of the rosemary. Layer the potato slices over the tomatoes, splash on more oil and bake for 30 minutes. Take the dish out of the oven.

Thoroughly wash the sardines, then remove the heads and the spines. Open them out and spread them across the potato slices in the baking dish.

Sprinkle on the parsley and oregano and a little salt. Layer the remaining slices of tomato over the sardines. Drizzle with more oil and sprinkle on the remaining rosemary, plus the pine nuts and breadcrumbs. Return the dish to the oven and bake for another 15 minutes. Just before serving, scatter the olives over. Serve warm.

Variations: As well as, or instead of the potatoes, you can create a layer of sliced zucchini (courgettes) or sliced eggplant (aubergine). You can also sprinkle a layer of parmesan cheese on top.

You can simplify the *tegame* into a Ligurian *zuppetta* ('little soup') called *bagnun*. Leave out the potatoes, the olives, the pine nuts, the rosemary and the breadcrumbs, but include a tablespoon of finely chopped carrot. Make a *sofregit* (see page 49) with onion, carrot, garlic and tomatoes, adding a splash of white wine when you are adding the garlic. After cooking the tomatoes for 10 minutes, add 6 sardine fillets (or three butterflied sardines) and the chopped oregano and parsley, then cook for another 10 minutes. Serve with toasted bread for dipping.

In Nice, they turn the *tian* into a kind of custard, baking layers of thinly sliced vegetables, and then covering them with a beaten mixture of milk and eggs (with a pinch of grated nutmeg) and baking for a further 20 minutes.

Poisson au four façon Pauline

(Whole baked fish with tomatoes, potatoes and olives)

We had this simple but impressive dish at Les Templiers restaurant in Collioure, where the waiter explained that it is named after Pauline Pous, the original chef, who supposedly served it to Picasso and various other artists during the 1920s. The name literally translates as 'fish in the oven Pauline-style'. The vegetable element of the recipe remains constant, but the fish that bakes on top of the vegetables varies with the catch of the day. The only requirement is that the fish be flat, because then it cooks more evenly and its juices run into the potatoes.

Warning: when you are filleting the baked fish, do not turn it over. Lift off the fillets from the top side of the fish, then pull the spine away from the bottom half and put the spine on another plate. The locals believe that if somebody turns a whole baked fish while serving it, somewhere in the Mediterranean a fishing boat overturns, and you don't want that on your conscience.

a good splash of olive oil
3 potatoes, peeled and
  thinly sliced
6 garlic cloves
4 bay leaves
1 fennel bulb, thinly sliced
sea salt and freshly
  ground black pepper

2 sprigs each of fresh
  thyme, oregano and
  rosemary
4 tomatoes, thinly sliced
2 zucchini (courgettes),
  thinly sliced
a handful of pitted
  black olives

1 large flat fish, such as
  sole, flounder, halibut
  or turbot, cleaned
  and scaled
curly endive salad,
  to serve

Preheat the oven to 200°C (400°F).

Splash some olive oil into a large baking dish, and put a layer of potato slices across the bottom of the dish, interspersed with the garlic cloves, bay leaves and fennel slices. Sprinkle with a little salt and pepper. Transfer to the oven and bake for 20 minutes.

Scatter the thyme, oregano and rosemary sprigs across the potato slices, and on top of them layer the tomato slices and a layer of zucchini. Scatter the olives over the vegetables, splash on more olive oil and bake for another 15 minutes.

Now put the whole fish on top. Cover with foil and bake for 15 minutes.

To serve, place the baking dish in the middle of the table. Gently lift the fish onto a large plate and fillet it, peeling back the skin from the spine and giving each guest a slice, lifting the spine away when you have served the top half of the fish. Give everyone large spoons so they can serve themselves vegetables from the baking dish.

Serve with a curly endive salad.

COLLIOURE (LES PAYS CATALANS):
The ancient craft of boat building
survives in the back streets of the
village, but on a smaller scale.

Picking up a piece of Picasso

S everal small Picassos used to hang in the bar of the Hotel Les Templiers in the village of Collioure, in south-western France. Young Pablo had given them to the hotel in exchange for meals, as did an assortment of other painters from the artists' colony that established itself in the area over the first three decades of the 20th century. Swapping visual art for culinary art is a time-honoured tradition in European restaurants.

But an evil customer stole one of the Picassos, causing René Pous, the owner of Les Templiers, to lock the other contributions away and replace them with a photo of the maestro standing next to him above a dedication: *Pour mon ami, René Pous. Pablo Picasso.* Plenty of other paintings still cover the walls of the bar and the adjoining hotel and restaurant, demonstrating the energy of an artists' colony that included the likes of André Derain, Georges Braque, Henri Matisse, and the Scottish designer Charles Rennie Mackintosh.

Apart from the art, the pretty village of Collioure has two other claims to fame: its anchovies and its identity.

The anchovies caught in these waters are said to be the best in France, and are sent all over Europe, as well as being sold in tins and jars in little blue shops throughout the town. Being the anchovy capital of France means having a very particular sense of humour. On the table in Les Templiers is a coaster imprinted with a riddle: *Pourquoi les anchois ne vont-ils en cours d'anglais? Parce que'ils sont fish.* (Why don't anchovies go to English classes? Because they are *poissons*.)

But we should not have described Collioure as the anchovy capital of France, because the residents do not identify as French. They are in *le pays Catalan*. To the bureacrats in Paris, Collioure is a village (population 3000) in the region of Languedoc-Roussillon. But to independence activists in Barcelona, Collioure is Cotlliure, a town in Catalunya Nord. The Catalan colours — red and yellow — hang everywhere. Shop signs say *Espadrilles, Tissus Catalans*; *Gourmet Catalan*; *Specialitée Catalane*; and *Nos tapas du moment*. The bookshop in the castle (built by the Knights Templar in 1345) sells a beautiful volume called *Cuisinière Catalane*, with recipes (in a mixture of French and Catalan) for the likes of *Trinxat au chou vert, Fideus aux gambas, Mar y muntanya, Escalivade, Sarzuela, Ouillade, Bunyettes* and *La fameuse sauce romesco*.

In restaurants, the wine lists include a section for *vin de pays Catalan*, which means, in particular, Banyuls, the sweet red which is said to be the only dessert wine that can stand up to chocolate.

So Collioure is like Nice: a border town, permanently in transition between two coastal cultures which are not, in the end, very different from each other — if this book has made its case.

COLLIOURE (LES PAYS CATALANS):
For most of the 20th century, artists
such as Picasso swapped paintings
for meals and drinks in the bar of
Les Templiers hotel.

Rougets de cassis *(Baked red mullet)*

This is our favourite Mediterranean fish, a seemingly infinite resource of sweet pink flesh all around the coastline in the right season. The English call them red mullet, the French call them *rouget*, the Catalans call them *moll*, the Ligurians call them *triglia* (pronounced 'treel-ya') and the Greeks call them *barbunya*. In the town of Tellaro, east of Genoa, they use them as a stuffing for ravioli. West of Genoa, *rougets à la Niçoise* are fried in oil and served on a bed of tomatoes with anchovies and lemon juice. In Tarragona, they fry them and serve with romesco sauce.

This is our interpretation of a dish we encountered in an excellent restaurant called Le Grand Bleu in the village of Cassis, near Marseille. We'd seen 'rougets' scrawled on a blackboard headed *Arrivage Permanent de Poissons Frais* ('Constant Arrival of Fresh Fish') and we had to take advantage of the moment.

We think their perfect accompaniment is potatoes.

1 garlic clove, finely chopped
8 basil leaves, chopped
125 ml (4 fl oz/½ cup) olive oil, plus extra for drizzling
1 kg (2 lb 4 oz) medium-sized red mullets, scaled and filleted, heads and bones reserved for the stock

4 large potatoes, peeled
2 large white onions, peeled and thinly sliced
sea salt and freshly ground black pepper
1 large tomato, peeled, seeded and sliced
60 ml (2 fl oz/¼ cup) white wine
1 tablespoon small capers, rinsed and chopped

For the stock
fish heads and bones from the red mullet (see left)
1 small onion, peeled and cut into wedges
2 celery stalks, roughly chopped
1 carrot, roughly chopped

First, make the stock. Thoroughly wash the reserved heads and bones of the mullet, then place them in a large heavy-based saucepan with the onion, celery and carrot. Cover with water and bring to the boil over medium heat, then lower the heat and simmer for 30 minutes. Strain the broth into a bowl, discarding the fish heads and bones.

Preheat the oven to 180°C (350°F). Oil a large baking dish.

In a large bowl, mix half the garlic and half the basil with the olive oil. Toss the fish fillets in that mixture, making sure they are thoroughly coated. Let them marinate while you prepare the potatoes.

Cut the potatoes into slices about 5 mm (¼ inch) thick. Cook them in a pot of boiling salted water for 8 minutes. Lift them out using a slotted spoon, placing them around the oiled baking dish.

Lay the onion slices on top of the potatoes. Season with salt and pepper and sprinkle with the rest of the basil. Spread on a layer of tomato slices, drizzle with more olive oil and sprinkle with the remaining garlic. Layer the marinated fish fillets over the top, and drizzle with any marinade remaining in the bowl.

Pour in the wine, then 125 ml (4 fl oz/½ cup) of the stock. (Freeze the remaining stock in a freezer-proof container to use next time, or in other recipes.)

Scatter with the capers and bake for 30 minutes, or until the fish is tender.

Carry the dish to the table and let everyone help themselves.

Brandacujun *(Salt cod and potato bake)*

We brushed briefly by baccala in earlier chapters — in a *brandade* on top of crostini in chapter 3, and in a trio of salads in chapter 4 — but now it's time to celebrate its full splendour. We like talking about baccala because it lets the Vikings join the story dominated so far by the Greeks, the Romans and the Arabs. Around 1000 years ago, the Vikings caught lots of cod in the north Atlantic and found a way to preserve it so they could sell it all around the Mediterranean.

When the people of Liguria, Provence and Catalunya ran short of fresh seafood in the winter, they applied their flavouring skills to the Viking product and generated a multitude of nourishing family feasts.

This recipe shows what they do with salt cod in the Riviera di Ponente — the half of Liguria that is west of Genoa. It makes the most of the local black olives and the local olive oil. The dialect name, *brandacujun*, comes from the old Provençal word *brandare*, meaning 'to shake', and the old Ligurian word *cujun*, meaning 'idiot'. The message is: any fool can cook this.

In Nice, they call this dish *estocaficada* — from *stoccafisso*, literally 'stickfish', because the Vikings sold the dried cod in the form of long strips that were as durable as their swords.

1 kg (2 lb 4 oz) baccala (salt cod), cut into chunks
700 g (1 lb 9 oz) potatoes, peeled and diced
3 bay leaves

1 garlic clove
5 flat-leaf (Italian) parsley sprigs, leaves picked
300 ml (10½ fl oz) olive oil

2 tablespoons small black olives (ideally Taggiasca), pitted
1 tablespoon pine nuts
ground white pepper

Soak the pieces of baccala for 48 hours, changing the water four times a day. Put the baccala, the potatoes and the bay leaves in a large saucepan, cover with water and bring to the boil for 30 minutes.

Drain the water off and let the mixture cool. Lift out the baccala pieces, put them on a wooden board, and, using your fingers and a fork, remove the skin and the bones. Break up the baccala into small pieces and put them back in the pan with the potatoes. Discard the bay leaves.

Chop the garlic and the parsley leaves together, very finely, and mix them in a bowl with the olive oil. Pour this mixture over the potatoes and the baccala and mix together well. Add the olives, pine nuts and a generous sneeze of white pepper. Mix thoroughly with a wooden spoon.

Vigorously shake — *brandare!* — the pot a few times, and serve warm. Keep any leftovers in the fridge; this dish will be just as good the next day.

Variations:
The Catalans spell the salt cod slightly differently (*bacallá*) and cook it a little differently too. They debone it, toss it in flour, fry it in oil and bake it with tomatoes and paprika to produce a dish they call *bacallá a la llauna* (literally 'on the tin'). Or they stir through chopped prunes and spinach as they are frying it to make *bacallá a la manresana*. Or they fry it in batter and drizzle it with a mixture of honey and vinegar to create a 'sweet and sour' sensation, *bacallá amb mel*.

CASSIS (PROVENCE):
The restaurants around
the port serve locally
caught seafood, and make
a fish soup that is simpler
than the *bouillabaisse* of
neighbouring Marseille.

Caille et figues *(Quail and figs)*

Chicken with figs and honey is a classic of inland Provence. We decided to adapt it slightly by using quail instead of chicken, and removing the honey because the figs, when cooked, are sweet enough. We Ligurianised it by using the ancient grain called farro instead of the rice the French would usually serve with it.

Farro comes in two forms — wholegrain and what the Italians call *semi-perlato*. If you've got the wholegrain version, you need to soak it overnight before cooking it. The semi-pearled version can be cooked straight away. Either way it's a nutty, chewy treat which the Romans thought helped a man stay potent into his nineties (the Viagra of its day, apparently).

Farro is a key ingredient in an eastern Ligurian dish called *gran pistau*, in which various grains are crushed and boiled in a chicken stock. And if that word *pistau* seems familiar, yes, we are back to the Latin origins of *pesto*, meaning 'pounded'.

8 quails
sea salt and freshly ground black pepper
2 rosemary sprigs, leaves picked and chopped
2 sage sprigs, leaves picked and finely chopped
125 ml (4½ fl oz/½ cup) olive oil

1 white onion, thinly sliced
1 garlic clove, finely chopped
60 ml (2 fl oz/¼ cup) white wine
1 teaspoon balsamic vinegar
1 tablespoon olive oil
8 large figs

For the farro
1 small quail, chopped up
1 white onion, cut into quarters
1 small carrot, roughly chopped
2 bay leaves
½ teaspoon sea salt
500 g (1 lb 2 oz) farro

You begin by cooking the farro in quail stock (or chicken stock if you want to shortcut the process). To make the quail stock, put the quail pieces in a large pot, along with the onion, carrot, bay leaves and salt. Cover with water and bring it to the boil. Lower the heat and simmer gently for 25 minutes. Lift out the quail pieces and when they have cooled, remove and discard the bones, putting the meat back into the stock. Add the farro and boil for another 25 minutes. Drain and set the farro aside.

Meanwhile, preheat the oven to 160°C (315°F).

Cut the quails in half using kitchen scissors, or a large heavy knife. Sprinkle salt, pepper, and the rosemary and sage over them.

Splash the olive oil into a heavy-based frying pan and place it over medium heat. Add the onion and fry for 5 minutes, then add the garlic and cook for another 3 minutes. Now add the quails, skin side down, and brown for 4 minutes.

Splash in the white wine and let the alcohol evaporate for 3 minutes, turning the quails at the same time.

Arrange the quails in a baking dish, sprinkling on any remaining sage and rosemary. Cover with foil and bake for 20 minutes.

Mix the balsamic vinegar with the oil. Cut the figs in half and coat them in the vinegar mixture. Turn the oven up to 200°C (400°F). Place the figs, cut side up, in the baking dish with the quails and bake, uncovered, for 5 minutes.

Divide the farro among four plates and dress with a little oil. Distribute the quails and the figs over the farro, pouring on any juices from the baking dish, and enjoy.

Llenties estofades
(Lentil and chorizo stew)

We couldn't leave Catalunya without recognising the historic importance of the pig, and of lentils as a supporting staple. Pork became a fad in the 16th century after the Spanish monarchy expelled the Jews and Moors, who had lived there harmoniously for centuries. People were desperate to prove to the Inquisition that they were loyal Christians, so they proceeded to hang pig parts in their houses and put pig parts in every second dish. Here we use the pig's foot, the pig's belly and the various other parts of the porcine anatomy that make up chorizo.

Lentils are another Greek gift to Catalunya — very healthy and a fine vehicle for carrying the flavours of whatever they are cooked with. Remnants of lentil meals, dated to 9000 years ago, have been found in what was Greek territory in Anatolia (modern Turkey). They might have flavoured them with garlic then, but certainly not peppers.

olive oil, for pan-frying
2 pig's trotters
150 g (5½ oz) pancetta (or bacon, if you can't find pancetta), finely chopped
4 small chorizo sausages
2 onions, finely chopped

2 green capsicums (bell peppers), diced
2 carrots, finely chopped
3 garlic cloves, finely chopped
3 large green chillies, kept whole
2 pinches of ground cumin

200 g (7 oz) ripe tomatoes, peeled, seeded and diced
500 g (1 lb 2 oz/2⅓ cups) small brown lentils
2 litres (70 fl oz/8 cups) chicken stock (page 22)
sea salt

Splash some olive oil into a high-sided frying pan over medium heat. Add the trotters and the pancetta and sizzle for 3 minutes, turning them now and then.

Chop the chorizos into pieces about 5 mm (¼ inch) thick, add them to the pan and mix thoroughly. Cook, stirring now and then, for about 5 minutes.

Add the onion, capsicum and carrot and cook for 5 minutes, then add the garlic and the whole green chillies and cook for another 3 minutes.

Now stir in the cumin and tomatoes. Turn the heat down to low, cover and cook for 30 minutes, shaking the pan regularly.

Stir in the lentils, then pour in the stock. Mix thoroughly, bring back to the boil, then lower the heat, cover and simmer gently for 30 minutes.

Taste for seasoning, adding salt if necessary. Scoop out the trotters, remove and discard the bones, then cut the meat into small pieces.

Serve the lentils on individual plates, topped with pieces of trotter.

GENOA (LIGURIA):
The Ligurians save elaborate
desserts for special occasions,
but don't mind a bite of
biscotti with their coffee.

Desserts & Pastries

NICE (PROVENCE):
The Cours Saleya, one block back from the waterfront in the Old Town of Nice, was where the wealthiest Italian residents lived in the 16th century, and became a fruit and flower market in 1861.

The Arab sweetening

The Catalans are legendary for their sweet tooths (teeth?), which is why most of the recipes in this chapter come from that region.

The Arabs started planting sugar cane (from India) in Spain in the 11th century, while the rest of Europe had to make do with expensive honey as the prime sweetener.

Europe's first known patisserie opened in Barcelona in 1382, and in the 1500s a Barcelona publisher produced a kind of cookbook called *Llibre de Totes Maneres de Confits* ('Book of All Kinds of Confectionery'). By 1585, when bitter chocolate arrived in Spain from the Americas, the Catalans had the choice of treating it as a savoury spice or as a confectionery, and of course they copped it sweet.

These days, the laneways of Barcelona, Tarragona and Girona are dotted with pastry shops from which the locals emerge, clutching golden parcels that ooze custard. Look for signs that say *Xurreria* or *Brioixeria*.

The Ligurians have more savoury tastes, finishing most meals with just fruit or cheese and confining confectionery consumption to special occasions — the feast days ordained by the Church. Around Christmas, for example, they have a tradition of bringing a fruit tart called *Spungata* (page 259) whenever they go visiting at afternoon teatime. At weddings they serve a marsala-soaked sponge called *sacripantina*, supposedly created in 1851.

The Provençals lean towards the Ligurian austerity, but when they go for sweets, they go big. At Christmas they have a tradition called *les treize desserts* ('the 13 desserts'), numbered in honour of Jesus and the Apostles. A fabulous spread is laid out on Christmas Eve, and is supposed to be gradually depleted over the next three days (between the usual seasonal excesses). There is no strict rule about what the 13 must be, but they usually include 'the four beggars' (dried figs, raisins, dates and walnuts), as well as oranges, apples, pears, winter melon, and cooked items such as fruit tarts, *beignets* (fried donuts), nougat, and *fougasse* flavoured with pralines and orange water. With the addition of various fruits and nuts, you could construct the 13 desserts of Christmas from this chapter. The Provençals wouldn't mind the odd Catalan contribution.

The big day for devotees of dessert is 19 March. It is dedicated to St Joseph (the father or foster-father of Jesus, depending on your allegiance), and it always falls during Lent, when devout Christians are not supposed to eat meat, but can consume any amount of sugar. The Catalans have allocated to Saint Joseph their *Bunyols* (fried donuts with aniseed, page 260), *Crèma Catalana* (page 266), and *Xuixo* (page 272). Girona has an annual procession called Marxa del Xuxo, which ends with the participants being handed *xuixos* prepared by the local guild of pastry chefs. That's what we call giving pudding its just desserts.

Le riz aux cerises

(Cherry and almond rice pudding)

The tiny town of Céret (pronounced 'serray'), in south-western France near the border with Spain, is where the first cherries of spring appear. By tradition, the best box of the first cherry harvest is sent to the Élysée Palace in Paris, for the personal consumption of Monsieur Le President. The cherries of Céret are so luscious they do not need a lot of creativity in any desert containing them, which is why the local signature dish is pretty plain — just rice (from the nearby Camargue, of course), cooked in milk with a little sugar and cinnamon.

Because you are unlikely to obtain cherries of Céret quality most of the year, we've adapted the recipe, replacing cow's milk with almond milk (which gives it a Catalan touch), and enriching it with eggs and mascarpone (which brings back France and introduces Italy). If you're able to obtain luscious fresh cherries, replace our tinned cherries with real ones.

1 litre (35 fl oz/4 cups) almond milk
1 vanilla bean, split lengthways, seeds scraped
1 cinnamon stick
1 teaspoon orange zest

165 g (5¾ oz/¾ cup) arborio or carnaroli rice
100 g (3½ oz) sugar
4 egg yolks
165 g (5¾ oz/⅔ cup) mascarpone

200 g (7 oz/1⅓ cups) fresh cherries, stones removed, or tinned cherries
100 g (3½ oz) almonds, roasted, then chopped

In a saucepan, combine the almond milk, the split vanilla bean and its seeds, the cinnamon stick, orange zest and the rice. Simmer for 20 minutes, stirring occasionally.

Once the rice is soft, remove the vanilla pod and cinnamon stick. Stir in the sugar and egg yolks, then cook over low heat for about 8 minutes, until the mixture has thickened.

Stir the mascarpone through. Push the cherries gently into the rice. Divide among bowls, and serve scattered with the chopped almonds.

Fichi secchi *(Sun-dried figs)*

This is a very simple recipe, which will take you a mere 96 hours. The Romans found figs in the eastern part of their empire, and spread them all through the west, making them an obsession in Spain and France for 2000 years. Figs are at their best in late summer, and best eaten fresh then, but as the cooler weather comes along, you might want to think about ways to enhance their flavour. Drying them brings out their sugar, and makes them more easily used in other recipes, such as the next one in this chapter.

12 ripe figs
sunshine

water
bay leaves

Try to use figs that are all equally ripe — soft to the touch, more purple than green.

Sit them in a flat basket, not touching each other, with the stalks pointing up. Leave them in the sun for 2 days, bringing them in at night, and covering them with a tea towel.

When the sun goes down on the second day, boil a pot of water, turn off the heat, and immerse the figs in the hot water for 2 minutes.

Put them back in the basket and leave them out in the sun for another 2 days.

Bring them back inside, put bay leaves between them, and keep them covered until you are ready to eat them.

Serve them with walnuts and almonds at the end of a heavy meal.

Biscotti *(Fig, almond and orange biscuits)*

Since the year 1666, the southern French town of Sète has been holding an annual jousting tournament on its canal, whereby longboat crews use wooden poles to push each other into the water, while drummers in the back of the boats help the rowers keep their rhythm. This August festival is celebrated for the rest of the year with the eating of boat-shaped biscuits called *navettes*.

Navettes come in many flavours and colours, so we thought we'd try to adapt a traditional Ligurian recipe to a boat shape. It didn't work. As you see in the photo, our navettes came out looking more like surfboards than jousting boats, so we decided to call them by the Ligurian name — *biscotti*. The making of navettes, we found, is best left to the bakeries of southern France.

180 g (6½ oz) butter, at room temperature
480 g (1 lb 1 oz) caster (superfine) sugar
1 teaspoon orange zest
6 eggs

600 g (1 lb 5 oz/4 cups) plain (all-purpose) flour
3 teaspoons baking powder
60 g (2¼ oz/heaped ½ cup) almond meal

a pinch of sea salt
180 g (6½ oz/1 cup) sun-dried figs (see page 253)
200 g (7 oz/1¼ cups) almonds

It's best to make the dough the day before, and refrigerate it overnight. Here's how: in a food processor, cream together the butter, sugar and orange zest. Add the eggs and pulse until creamy. In a bowl, stir together the flour, the baking powder, almond meal and salt. Add the mixture from the food processor and, with your hands, slowly knead it all together to form a dough. Finely chop the figs and the almonds and add them to the dough. Cover with plastic wrap and refrigerate overnight.

On the day you are making the biscuits, mould the dough into five logs, then refrigerate for at least 20 minutes, while preheating the oven to 160°C (315°F).

Place the logs on an oiled baking tray and bake for about 15 minutes, or until golden brown. Take them out of the oven and leave to cool a little. Turn the oven down to 100°C (200°F).

Slice the logs on an angle, into oval biscuits about 1 cm (½ inch) thick. Arrange the biscuits on two or three oiled baking trays lined with baking paper and dry them out in the oven for about 10 minutes, until firm.

To check the firmness, remove one biscuit and let it cool for 2 minutes. If it snaps, it's ready, and you can take the others out.

They will stay fresh in an airtight container at room temperature for up to 2 weeks.

LE COMPTOIR DE
CHOCOLATERIE MATHILDE
Maison de Qualité
COMESTIBLES
CHOCOLATS
MAISON
THÉS
CAFÉS
Biscuits
LIQUEURS
APÉRITIFS
Spécialité
PÂTE
À TARTINER
de Mathilde
CHOCOLATS
MAISON
CONFISERIES
GUIMAUVES
BISCUITS
Douceurs
pour les petits
et les grands
VENTE AU
DÉTAIL
GROS et
SEMI GROS
EXIGEZ
la
Marque
LE COMPTOIR DE
MATHILDE
MÉFIEZ VOUS
DES
CONTREFAÇONS!
ON PORTE
EN
VILLE
Comptoir de
MATHILDE NICE

NICE (PROVENCE):
The sweet shop called
Le Comptoir de Mathilde
('Matilda's counter') looks
200 years old, but actually
opened in 2001, then spread
throughout France.

Spungata *(Ligurian apricot tart)*

In the eastern Ligurian winter, *spungata* is a pastry which a well-mannered guest brings along when invited to afternoon tea or coffee at a friend's place. It brings good luck for the year to come. That's been the case in Lucio's neighbourhood for 1000 years — possibly much longer, since there are ancient Roman recipes that sound very similar, and all the modern ingredients would have been available 2000 years ago.

These days most spungatas are store-bought (beautifully wrapped), and sometimes, we suspect, they stay in a cupboard of the household to which they've been gifted until that household is about to visit somebody else.

We hope our recipe will smell so beautiful during the baking that you'll want to eat it straight away.

350 g (12⅓ oz/2 cups) dried apricots	750 g (26½ oz/5 cups) plain (all-purpose) flour	2 tablespoons pine nuts, chopped
a sprinkling of ground cinnamon	sea salt	60 g (2 oz) blanched almonds, finely chopped
3 eggs	450 g (16 oz) butter, at room temperature	90 g (3 oz) candied fruits, chopped
200 g (7 oz) sugar		

Simmer the dried apricots for 20 minutes with a generous pinch of ground cinnamon. Remove them from the water, let them cool, then mash them into a jam and set aside.

Beat the eggs and mix them with the sugar.

On a clean flat surface, make a mound of the flour. Add a pinch of salt. Make a well in the middle of the flour and pour in the egg mixture. With your hands, mix in the butter and make a firm dough. If it seems dry, add 1 tablespoon water. Let the dough rest for 30 minutes.

Preheat the oven to 180°C (350°F). In a bowl, mix the mashed apricots with the pine nuts, almonds and candied fruits. Set aside.

Divide the dough into two balls, one slightly bigger than the other. With a rolling pin, roll the bigger one into a disc that can cover the bottom and sides of a greased 30 cm (12 inch) round tart (flan) tin. Roll out the other ball into a smaller disc and set aside.

Spread the fruit and nut mixture over the bottom layer of dough, spreading it evenly. Rest the top layer of dough over the top and press down around the edges; slice off any overlapping dough. Bake for 30 minutes.

Take the pie out of the oven and leave for at least 30 minutes before serving. Spungata is best served lukewarm, with cream or ice cream.

Bunyols / Beignets *(Aniseed donuts)*

We get into another name game here. Are the fried puffs called *bunyols* in Catalunya the same as the fried puffs called *beignets* in Provence and *zeppoli* in Liguria? All were traditionally served around Easter time, with the Niçois enjoying an elaborate version (flavoured with orange flower water) on Mardi Gras, the Tuesday before the austerity of Lent. The Catalans nibbled a version called *bunyols de vent* (fritters of wind) during the 40 days of fasting, as a way to fill up while they were not allowed to eat meat.

Outside of Easter, a savoury version of *bunyol* is often made with salt cod. Here is the sweet version, usually flavoured with aniseed — though you can replace that with any sweet liqueur you like, even including orange.

2 tablespoons fennel seeds
70 g (2½ oz) caster
 (superfine) sugar,
 plus extra for dusting
1 teaspoon lemon zest
70 g (2½ oz) butter,
 diced

390 ml (14 fl oz) milk
10 g (¼ oz) active
 dried yeast
3 eggs
100 ml (3½ fl oz) aniseed
 liqueur, such as pastis,
 sambuca or ouzo

600 g (1 lb 5 oz/4 cups)
 plain (all-purpose)
 flour
5 g (⅛ oz) baking powder
a pinch of sea salt
sunflower or vegetable
 oil, for deep-frying

Toast the fennel seeds by tossing them in a dry frying pan over medium heat for 2 minutes. Blitz in a spice grinder and set aside.

In a small saucepan, combine the sugar, lemon zest, butter and 90 ml (3 fl oz) of the milk and bring to a boil. When the butter has melted, pour the mixture into a bowl. Add the remaining milk, then add the yeast and mix it through. After about 5 minutes, once the yeast has started to bubble, whisk in the eggs and aniseed liqueur.

In a mixing bowl fit for an electric mixer, combine the flour, baking powder, salt, 1 teaspoon of the ground fennel seeds, and the egg mixture. Using a paddle or dough hook, beat for about 2 minutes, until you have a sticky dough.

Grease a large bowl with cooking oil. Scrape the dough into the bowl, cover with plastic wrap and allow the dough to rest for 30 minutes, or until doubled in size.

Heat about 6 cm (2½ inches) of oil in a deep frying pan or wok over medium heat for 3 minutes, then reduce the heat a little.

Take one-third of the doughnut mixture and place in a piping (icing) bag with no nozzle. Squeeze out a little at a time and, using scissors, cut golfball-sized lumps off the end, dropping them carefully into the hot oil.

Fry for about 3 minutes or until golden, spinning them around in the hot oil for an even colour. The *bunyols* will double in size. Be careful not to heat the oil too much, otherwise the bunyols will be raw inside and brown on the outside.

Drain briefly on paper towel. Dust with the remaining ground fennel seeds and a little extra caster sugar. Serve warm.

Xurros *(Tube donuts with chocolate sauce)*

Strictly speaking, xurros were not a Catalan invention. The idea of making donuts this way is supposed to have been brought to Europe by the Portuguese, who saw something like it during their first visits to China in the 16th century. They were rapidly embraced throughout Spain.

The citizens of Barcelona eat and drink late, and then, around 2 am, resort to xurros from street stalls as a potential hangover cure. They are very effective, in our experience. To make these xurros look like the Barcelona version, you will need a piping bag with a fluted nozzle.

60 g (2¼ oz) butter
1 tablespoon caster (superfine) sugar
a pinch of sea salt
300 g (10½ oz/2 cups) plain (all-purpose) flour
zest of ½ orange
1 egg yolk

vegetable oil, for deep-frying

For the chocolate sauce
150 g (5½ oz/1 cup) dark chocolate
18 g (¾ oz) cornflour (cornstarch)
15 g (½ oz) sugar

½ teaspoon orange zest
300 ml (10½ fl oz) milk

For dusting
110 g (3¾ oz/½ cup) sugar
1 teaspoon ground cinnamon

Put the chocolate sauce ingredients in a saucepan, whisk over low heat, then bring up to the boil and take off the heat. Keep in a warm place, or gently reheat just before serving.

In a small saucepan, bring the butter and 400 ml (14 fl oz) water up to the boil. Add the sugar, salt, flour and orange zest. Stir over low heat until the mixture forms a dough.

Continue to cook on low heat, stirring constantly, for about 5 minutes, until the dough leaves a coating on the base of the pan. The dough must be dry and not too soft.

Transfer the dough to a food processor and, with the motor running, add the egg yolk. Spoon the mixture into a piping (icing) bag fitted with a 2 cm (¾ inch) diameter fluted nozzle.

Pour cooking oil into a large saucepan to a depth of 8 cm (3 inches). Heat the oil over medium heat and after about 2 minutes, drop a small piece of dough into it. If it sizzles and turns gold, the oil is at the right temperature. If it turns brown, the oil is too hot and the saucepan should be removed from the heat for a minute; you want the oil to be sitting at around 170°C (325°F).

Using a pair of scissors to cut the dough, pipe the xurros as 10 cm (4 inch) tubes into the hot oil, working in batches so you don't overcrowd the pan. Cook for 2 minutes, using a fork to turn the xurros over in the hot oil. Once they are golden brown, use a slotted spoon to transfer them onto a plate lined with paper towel.

Roll the xurros in the combined sugar and cinnamon. Serve hot, with the warm chocolate sauce for your guests to dip them into.

The sweet secret
behind the Costa Brava

T here are lots of little lanes and courtyards in Girona. Arya Stark ran through most of them in *Game of Thrones*. But the only one that needs to concern us here is the one that runs off Carrer de la Cort Reial, because it contains a pastry shop called Montse l'Artesana, which perfectly manifests the Catalan crush on sweet delights. A red-haired young woman, who should be a character in *Game of Thrones*, stands behind a transparent panel and shouts instructions to a chef (from Madrid, so treated somewhat sceptically by the Catalans), who spends all day deep-frying the round aniseed dumplings called *Bunyols* (page 260) and the tubular donuts called *Xurros* (page 263).

Girona is 40 kilometres inland from the coast, so perhaps it should not be in this book. It has no Greek origins, being first a Roman fortress, then Visigoth, then Moorish. The Moors brought almonds, hazelnuts, oranges and cane sugar, so Girona's love of pastries and sweets is hardly surprising.

But we've included it for two reasons. Firstly, its food is more genuinely Catalan than Barcelona's, which has become so dependent on tourism that it plays up to every Spanish stereotype a visitor might expect; Girona (population 100,000) doesn't mind a bit of tourism, but it's not about to compromise its culture to attract it. Secondly, Girona is the ideal base from which to explore the Costa Brava.

Because you're a serious scholar, your first venture out of Girona should be to Empúries, the remains of what was probably the first major Greek settlement in Spain. In 575 BC, the Greeks (from Anatolia) fenced off an *emporion* (shopping centre) and started swapping their pottery for local foodstuffs. The trade was so successful, the settlement that came to be called Emporion grew into the largest Greek colony in Spain. The Romans arrived 400 years later, and started their own town up the hill. Roman writers at the time complained about the smell drifting up from the stone vats where the Greeks were making fish sauce out of the rotting innards of tuna, but they let Emporion remain independent until the war between Julius Caesar and Pompey in 49 BC, when it backed the wrong leader.

On the beach in front of the tanks where the fish sauce was made, you can picture oarsmen jumping ashore from their galleys as you eat the excellent tomato bread (page 70, which the Greeks would not have experienced) and sardines (which they would've) in a snack bar called La Terrassa del Moll Grec (Terrace of the Greek Port). In summer, you can go surfing with the Greek ghosts.

You should head down the coast for dinner in the Hotel Aigua Blava, to experience the Catalan highlight *Mar i muntanya* ('Sea and mountain'; page 222). The Aigua Blava version is half a chicken and half a lobster, enriched with a picada of almonds, hazelnuts, saffron and garlic, which makes surf and turf seem entirely logical.

Naturally, you'd head back to Girona for dessert.

EMPÚRIES (CATALUNYA): Behind the trees is the beach where Greek traders made their first landing in Spain 2600 years ago. On the beach nowadays is a café serving sardines, anchovies and tomato bread (which the Greeks could not have eaten).

Crèma Catalana *(Toffee-topped custard)*

We hate to diminish any Catalan achievement, but we might have to credit the French with the idea of burning sugar on top of a rich custard. A recipe very similar to this appears, under the name *crème brûlée*, in a French cookbook published in 1691. In the 19th century the English started calling it 'Trinity pudding' because it was a speciality of the chef at Trinity College, Cambridge. The French confuse the issue by referring to the custard under the topping as *crème anglaise* ('English cream', though it's unlikely to have been an Anglo invention).

What the Catalans did was add orange zest to a recipe that was originally flavoured only with vanilla, which was an inspiration because the sharpness of the orange cuts through the richness of the custard. They declared it to be one of the meatless dishes to be eaten on Saint Joseph's Day (March 19). Their name for it is *crema cremada* ('cremated cream').

The best way to serve this dish is immediately after the sugar has been caramelised, to maximise the contrast between hot crunchy toffee and cool smooth custard. But it's almost as good served at room temperature later that day. Originally the sugar on top of the custard was turned into toffee by the application of a hot iron. Please do not attempt this at home, if you intend ever to press your clothes again.

700 ml (24 fl oz) thin
  (pouring) cream
125 ml (4 fl oz/½ cup) milk
1 cinnamon stick
1 vanilla bean, split
  lengthways, seeds scraped

3 teaspoons lemon zest
3 teaspoons orange zest
8 egg yolks
125 g (4½ oz/heaped
  ½ cup) caster
  (superfine) sugar

For the topping
75 g (2½ oz/⅓ cup) caster
  (superfine) sugar

Preheat the oven to 140°C (275°F). Place two large ramekins, each about 450 ml (16 fl oz) capacity, in a baking dish lined with a tea towel.

In a saucepan, combine the cream, milk, cinnamon stick, vanilla bean pods and seeds, and the lemon and orange zest. Bring to the boil, then remove from the heat and allow to infuse for 10 minutes. Strain through a fine sieve, into a clean saucepan.

In a large heatproof bowl, mix together the egg yolks and the sugar until creamy. Bring the milk and cream back up to the boil, then pour it onto the egg yolks, one-third at a time, whisking well. Strain the mixture through a fine-mesh sieve, into a jug.

Three-quarters fill the ramekins with the mixture, then place the baking dish on a shelf in the oven. Finish filling the ramekins to just below the tops, then pour hot water into the baking dish, to come halfway up the sides of the ramekins. Bake for about 30 minutes, until the custards are set, with a slight wobble in the centre.

Remove the ramekins from the baking dish and let them cool at room temperature for 20 minutes, before putting them in the fridge for a few hours.

Evenly coat the top of each crèma catalana with the sugar, then caramelise lightly under a hot grill (broiler) — or with a kitchen blowtorch, if you have one — until golden brown. Serve immediately, or at room temperature. Give one of your guests the privilege of cracking the surface and serving the others.

Note: You could also pour the crèma catalana mixture into six smaller ramekins, and bake the custards for only about 12 minutes, until there is a slight wobble in the centre.

Tourte de blette *(Chard tart)*

This pie is an intriguing blend of sweet and savoury. It contains the giant leaves sometimes mistaken for spinach and variously known as silverbeet, mangold or Swiss chard (though they seem to have originated way south of Switzerland). It clearly has ancient origins: a tart made with *blettes* was described in a book called *Le Ménagier de Paris*, written in 1393. It's traditionally sliced into rectangles and served by itself as an afternoon snack, but we found it worked well as a dessert with mascarpone after a light meal … so, not *daube de boeuf*, then.

100 g (3½ oz) raisins

2 tablespoons brandy

500 g (1 lb 2 oz) silverbeet (Swiss chard) stalks

sea salt

3 apples

30 ml (1 fl oz) olive oil

3 tablespoons caster (superfine) sugar

2 eggs

40 g (1½ oz/½ cup) finely grated parmesan cheese

120 g (4¼ oz/¾ cup) pine nuts, toasted

cooking oil spray

1 teaspoon icing (confectioner's) sugar

For the dough

500 g (1 lb 2 oz/3⅓ cups) plain (all-purpose) flour

3 teaspoons baking powder

a pinch of sea salt

120 g (4¼ oz) caster (superfine) sugar

50 g (1¾ oz/½ cup) almond meal

2 eggs

80 ml (2½ fl oz/⅓ cup) olive oil

1 teaspoon lemon zest

In a bowl, soak the raisins in the brandy and set aside.

To make the dough, combine the flour, baking powder, salt, sugar and almond meal in a bowl. Make a well in the centre. In another bowl, whisk together the eggs, olive oil, lemon zest and 75 ml (2½ fl oz/⅓ cup) water. Pour the egg mixture into the well and incorporate to form a slightly crumbly dough. If the dough is too dry, work in a little more water. Bring together into a ball, cover with plastic wrap and allow to rest for 1 hour.

While the dough rests, remove the leaves from the silverbeet stalks. Bring a large pot of boiling water up to the boil with a small handful of salt. Add the silverbeet leaves and cook for 5 minutes. Drain, then quickly cool off under cold running water to stop the silverbeet cooking further. Once cool, put the leaves in a tea towel, roll up and wring out the excess water. Slice the silverbeet leaves and set aside.

Peel and core the apples, then cut them into cubes. Heat up a saucepan with the olive oil, toss in the diced apple and cook over medium heat for about 5 minutes, until soft. Stir in the sugar, then the raisins and brandy. Cook for 5 minutes.

In a bowl, whisk together the eggs and parmesan. Add the cooked silverbeet, the apple, raisins and pine nuts and stir them through.

Heat the oven to 170°C (325°F). Spray a 20 x 30 cm (8 x 12 inch) baking dish, at least 3 cm (1 inch) deep, with cooking oil.

Roll half the dough out between two sheets of baking paper, then line the baking dish with the pastry, making sure the pastry goes up the sides. Pour in the filling.

Roll the second pastry portion between two sheets of baking paper, and use it to cover the top of the pie, sealing the edges together.

Pierce the top pastry sheet using scissors, making small notches.

Place in the oven and bake for 50 minutes, or until the pie is amber in colour.

Let it cool, then sprinkle with the icing sugar. Cut it into squares and serve warm with whipped cream, or at room temperature for afternoon tea.

CAMOGLI (LIGURIA):
At lunchtime, the local
speciality is linguine
with pesto; for dinner,
it's octopus pie.

Xuixo *(Custard puffs)*

Xuixo (pronounced 'shoo-sho') is a custard-stuffed pastry that originated in the elegant city of Girona and became a favourite street food in Barcelona. Mid-morning and mid-afternoon you can see citizens strolling with paper-wrapped *xuixos* in their hands, trying not to squeeze the filling onto their shirts. The name is supposed to sound like a sneeze, in honour of its alleged inventor, a clown named El Tarlà. He was visiting the daughter of a pastry chef and hid in a big bag of flour when her father came home early. He was discovered when he started sneezing, and the only way he could avoid the father's wrath was to give him the recipe for a new kind of pastry. We've simplified El Tarlà's recipe, but the possibility of custard spillage if you squeeze them too zealously remains.

cooking oil spray
plain (all-purpose) flour,
  for dusting
vegetable oil, for deep-
  frying

For the custard
500 ml (17 fl oz/2 cups)
  milk
½ teaspoon lemon zest

¼ teaspoon orange zest
1 vanilla bean,
  split lengthways,
  seeds scraped
5 egg yolks
90 g (3¼ oz) caster
  (superfine) sugar
30 g (1 oz/¼ cup)
  cornflour (cornstarch)
20 g (¾ oz) butter

For the dough
150 ml (5 fl oz) milk
15 g (½ oz) butter
35 g (1¼ oz) caster
  (superfine) sugar
3 g (⅛ oz) dried yeast
1 egg
270 g (9½ oz) plain
  (all-purpose) flour
4 g (⅛ oz) baking powder

To make the custard, warm the milk, the lemon and orange zest, and the vanilla bean pod and seeds in a small saucepan until the mixture just comes to the boil, then take off the heat and leave to infuse for 10 minutes.

In a bowl, cream the egg yolks and sugar using electric beaters, then fold the cornflour through. Bring the infused milk up to the boil again.

Using a fine sieve, strain the milk into the egg yolks. Mix well, then pour the mixture into a clean saucepan over medium heat. Using a wooden spoon, stir constantly for about 5 minutes, or until the custard has boiled and thickened. Stir in the butter, mixing well. Leave to cool in the fridge for about an hour before deep-frying the *xuixo*.

To make the dough, bring the milk, butter and sugar to the boil in a small saucepan. Allow to cool to room temperature, before adding the yeast. After about 5 minutes, once the yeast has started to bubble, whisk in the egg.

In the bowl of an electric mixer, combine the flour and baking powder. Add the yeasty milk mixture. Using a dough hook or paddle, beat for about 3 minutes to form a dough. Scrape the dough into a large bowl sprayed with cooking oil. Cover with plastic wrap and rest for 30 minutes, until doubled in size. Firm in the fridge for 20 minutes.

Flour a bench, using lots of flour. Using a rolling pin, roll the dough out to a rectangle about 5 mm (¼ inch) thick. Using a blunt edge, a knife or pizza cutter, cut the dough into 8 cm (3 inch) squares. Transfer the cut pieces to a floured tray. Reroll the pastry scraps and cut out more pastry squares. Leave to rest on the tray for a further 10 minutes.

In a deep saucepan, bring 5 cm (2 inches) vegetable oil to 180°C (350°F) over medium heat. (If, after 2 minutes, a piece of dough dropped into the oil sizzles and starts to turn golden, the temperature is right.) In batches, fry the *xuixos* for 3–4 minutes each side, until golden and puffed. Remove using a slotted spoon and drain on paper towel.

Once slightly cool, pierce a hole in the centre of the *xuixos* on one side, and pipe in the cold custard, filling the space. Serve immediately.

Mel i mató

(Homemade ricotta with walnuts and honey)

This was served to us in the venerable restaurant Los Caracoles ('The Snails') in Barcelona — home-made cheese with crunchy walnuts scattered round the plate, and a glass half-filled with honey for pouring. We wondered how hard it would be to make cheese at home and we discovered that it's not hard at all, as long as you have patience. You need to let the liquid drip out of the curds for at least 48 hours to ensure the texture is firm enough to mould and slice.

Many cheeses are fermented with rennet — an enzyme from the stomach of a cow. Ours is fermented with lemon and buttermilk, making it suitable for vegetarians.

2 litres (70 fl oz/8 cups)
  milk, organic and
  unhomogenised
  if possible

500 ml (17 fl oz/2 cups)
  buttermilk
2 teaspoons lemon
  juice

top-quality honey,
  for drizzling
50 g (1¾ oz) walnuts,
  roasted

In a large saucepan, combine the milk, buttermilk and the lemon juice. Gently warm the milk over low heat, stirring occasionally to prevent scorching.

Leave to simmer for 30 minutes, but do not let the milk boil. The mixture will begin to separate and form small curds and a watery whey.

Now let the milk sit undisturbed at room temperature until cool.

Line a strainer with muslin (cheesecloth) and set it over a bowl. Once the milk is cool, carefully pour or spoon the curds through the cheesecloth, allowing the whey to drain away.

Leaving it sitting over the bowl, refrigerate the ricotta overnight for a firmer texture. The final texture of the cheese will depend on the draining time, with longer draining giving a firmer, drier result.

Store the ricotta in the fridge and use within 1 week.

Before serving, drizzle with honey and scatter roasted walnuts on top.

How to follow the Greeks, the Romans & the authors

The bookends of this story are two Roman amphitheatres: one in the ruined city of Luni, in eastern Liguria, and the other in the thriving city of Tarragona, in southern Catalunya. Lucio grew up near Luni, riding his bicycle over the ruins, so our journey should begin there …

1 BOCCA DI MAGRA

The name Bocca di Magra, a fishing village on the border of Liguria and Tuscany, means 'mouth of the Magra River'. At the spot where the river enters the sea, Lucio's family built a shack on the sand, back in 1950, and it grew into a huge restaurant called Capannina Ciccio (ristoranteciccio.it/it). That's where you can linger over seafood while you plan your travels. You would need to rent a car to see this neighbourhood properly (best to fly into Pisa airport and pick up the car there), and you should use it to visit the Luni ruins and amphitheatre (but please don't ride over them!), as well as the marble quarries of Carrara and the pretty villages of Monte-marcello and Tellaro (where D. H. Lawrence lived for a couple of years, telling a friend how a giant octopus used to emerge from the sea to ring the churchbell as a warning when pirates were approaching).

2 CINQUE TERRE

The five villages of the Cinque Terre are best visited on foot, so leave the car at La Spezia station, buy a Cinque Terre card and take the train to the first of the five, Riomaggiore. Have a look around, then walk to the next towns, Manarola and Corniglia. When you get to Vernazza, have lunch in the Gambero Rosso restaurant in the tiny port (ristorantegamberorosso.net/it), then take the train to the final town of Monterosso, which has a pleasant beach where you can swim. If you're there in summer, you can take a ferry back from Monterosso to Riomaggiore, observing the terraced vineyards draped over the cliffs, and then board the train to your car in La Spezia.

3 CAMOGLI

The Riviera towns between the Cinque Terre and Genoa are all pretty (and Portofino is very expensive), but we think the most interesting is Camogli, because of the *trompe l'oeil* paintings on the buildings. You should try the *trofie* with pesto at Pasta Fresca Fiorella on the waterfront. For dinner, continue to Recco, much less pretty because it was heavily bombed during World War II, where Manuelina (manuelina.it) offers *cappon magro* and cheese-stuffed focaccia.

4 GENOA

The little lanes of Genoa are crammed with shops selling focaccia and *farinata* (the chickpea pancake the Niçois call *socca*). One fine example is Da Franz & Co, at 81 Via Struppa. For freshly made pesto, try Il Genovese (ilgenovese.com). Its owner, Roberto Panizza, is a founder of the Palatafini Association, which organises the biannual competition to find the best handmade pesto in the world. And go to the seaside town of Varazze, west of Genoa, to try the *brandacujun* at Il Mulino (ilmulinovarazze.it/).

5 NICE

You could leave the car in Genoa and take the train round to Nice, where you should visit the flower market in Cours Saleya, any day but Monday, to see the array of vegetables that contribute to Provençal food. To eat that food, do lunch at the *socca* specialist Chez Pipo (chezpipo.fr) and dinner at the *petits farcis* and *daube de boeuf* specialist Lu Fran Calin at 5 Rue Francis Gallo in the Old Town.

About a 40-minute drive west of Nice is the town of St-Paul-de-Vence, where the spectacular La Colombe d'Or restaurant (la-colombe-dor.com/indexEN.html) has been making *pinzimonio* with anchovy sauce and swapping meals for paintings since 1920.

6 CASSIS

Cassis is the last train stop before Marseille, and it's worth getting out there for lunch at Le Grand Bleu restaurant (visit-cassis-360.com/le_grand_bleu.html) and then taking a boat ride around the limestone cliffs called Les Calanques.

7 MARSEILLE

Go to Le Vieux Port to stand on the spot where Greeks landed, and to visit the nearby museum of Greek bits and pieces. With the culture out of the way, check out the Saladin spice shop at 10 Rue Longue des Capucins. While you're in that neighbourhood, try a casual fish canteen called Toinou Les Fruits de Mer at 3 Cours St Louis (toinou.com). Choose your seafood from their display and the accompaniments you want, and they'll bring it to your table.

La Brasserie du Port — L'OM Café (25 Quai des Belges) serves a decent fish soup if you're in a hurry, but for the full bouillabaisse experience, you'll need to catch a cab or a bus around to Le Rhul (hotel-restaurant-le-rhul.com).

8 SÈTE

Everything in Sète happens on the canal. Go to La Méditerranéenne at 3 Quai Maximin Licciardi (la-mediterraneenne-sete.com) for a pretty good example of *macaronade* and other strange local maritime specialties. Much better is the dining room of the Grand Hôtel (legrandhotelsete.com/en/restaurant), which does an impeccable *bourride*. Catch the train next morning to Collioure.

9 COLLIOURE

Artists such as Picasso and Matisse ate at Les Templiers (hotel-templiers.com) and so should you. The colours, the signs and the shopping opportunities reveal you are in French Catalonie.

10 GIRONA

The train from Collioure to Girona takes about 2 hours. After visiting the cathedral, grab *bunyols* from the *xurreria* Montse l'Artesana (montse-lartesana.blogspot.com.au), and hire a car to explore the Costa Brava (arranging to leave it in Barcelona). If you're a Dalí-phile, go to Cadaqués, then work your way down the coast to the Greek ruins at Empúries and tomato bread on the beach. Finish in Aigua Blava, eating *mar i muntanya* in the hotel (hotelaiguablava.com/en).

11 BARCELONA

For Catalan dinner classics that have barely changed in 200 years, try Can Culleretes (culleretes.com). That's your first night out of the way. Next morning, head to the Boqueria market on La Rambla to see Catalan ingredients in all their glory, and do tapas at Quiosc Modern (no phone, no website, you just have to find it in the middle of the markets). Other excellent tapas can be found at El Xampanyet, Carrer de Montcada 22, and at La Cova Fumada, Carrer del Baluard 56.

You can indulge your sweet tooth at one of the three Escribà pastry shops (escriba.es). The one at Rambla de les Flors 83 does a fine *crèma catalana*.

12 TARRAGONA

Take the train down the Costa Daurada to the Roman province of Tarraconensis. For the definitive *fideua* and paella, visit Cal Joan (tarragonaturisme.cat/en/restaurant/cal-joan).

Walk through and around the amphitheatre to see the plantings of Roman herbs and fruits and reflect that 2000 years ago, there were soldiers, sailors and traders who — like you — had walked here and compared it with the other bookend, across the sea in Luni.

BOCCA DI MAGRA (LIGURIA):
This boy sits outside Capannina
Ciccio, the restaurant Lucio's
family built on the beach, gazing
out to sea as Lucio did between
shifts as the youngest waiter.

Lucio's conclusion

So here I was, in my early 60s, finally discovering the cuisine of my neighbours and finding out what they have in common with my Liguria. To start the process, I had to go back in time to when I was growing up in a little fishing village called Bocca di Magra.

I could say I was born into a family of restaurateurs, but that really meant a family who built a shack by the sea and in the summertime enjoyed cooking the catch of the day for friends and customers (who became friends!). In the winter, my parents and my aunt and uncle closed the restaurant and went back to a farming life further inland, with a different diet to what was served at Capannina Ciccio.

I feel very lucky to have grown up in these two different worlds. I have always eaten, with great curiosity and great pleasure, the food of any region. I learned at an early age to appreciate the quality of the ingredients, and as I travelled as an adult I came to appreciate any cuisine that is rich in culture and tradition, that satisfies both the palate and the soul. In my travels through Italy, I kept finding new cultures and cuisines in each new region.

Back then, we were a small group of children, playing in the rocky hills above the sea, while our parents were busy in the restaurant. I can still smell the aroma of the Ligurian herbs growing wild … rosemary, thyme, oregano, which we gathered for the restaurant. In the forest we found pine nuts for our mothers to make pesto. I could detect these two strong aromas, the wild herbs and pine nuts, in the olive oil that was splashed onto the slices of bread that were our afternoon snacks.

Some mornings I used to go with my mother to the village dock, waiting for the fishermen to float in, after being out at sea for most of the night. First to come in were the anchovy boats. People bought most of the anchovies on the dock to preserve under salt or to eat fresh in the stew we called *tian*. Next to arrive were the calamari and cuttlefish boats, my mother's favourite. The fishermen's wives would put the unsold fish into the baskets on their bikes and head inland to sell them door to door around the valley and in the hills.

Back at the restaurant, my mother would prepare our lunch. She would slice some leftover meat or fish or salami, put it in a large bowl with capers, vegetables, lettuce, tomatoes, anchovies and eggs, and dress the mixture with olive oil, vinegar and sometimes pesto. We'd eat it with fresh bread, sometimes toasted.

I didn't know at the time I was eating what my neighbours around the coastline would call a salad niçoise. But it came back to me as I began my trip along this beautiful coast with its recurring images: olive trees, vineyards, pine forests, colourful villages, solitary houses, fishing boats.

I had been to Provence and Catalunya before, more interested in architecture, art and landscape than food at the time. How fascinating is the process of discovery, not only for the pleasure of the palate but also for the excitement of becoming part of a new culture. I realised that what unites these three regions is the olive oil, garlic, herbs, anchovies and the use of mortar and pestle.

My co-author, David, started his explorations on the Italian side and worked his way around to Tarragona, south of Barcelona. I started in Barcelona and worked my way around to my birthplace in eastern Liguria. These are some of my strongest memories from my journey …

CATALUNYA

As soon as I arrived in Barcelona, I realised this is a city for the people, whether residents or visitors — people who love other people, people who love to share their life with others. We were lucky to have a room overlooking the Ramblas. I was fascinated watching all these people walking up and down and shopping at food kiosks that give people a welcome to … life. There one can find a selection of different prosciutto, salami and sausages, as well as the incredibly simple *pa amb tomaquet* — slices of dry bread, sprinkled with olive oil and salt and rubbed with squeezed tomatoes — and the *coca*, a focaccia type of bread, topped with vegetables. (The best version, I think, is with *escalivada* — roasted capsicum and eggplant.)

The best way to appreciate the food of Barcelona is to visit the La Boqueria market, a temple of Catalan gastronomy full of people shopping, eating, meeting friends, having a chat over a glass of wine, taking photos, enjoying life. I saw a stall displaying broad beans — the young fresh ones first in season. They were the best I had seen in my life (and I had grown up eating them every spring in Liguria). We bought a kilogram and took them to an outdoor table where we ordered some manchego cheese, some jamón and two glasses of white wine. We started podding these beautiful broad beans and slowly eating them with the cheese and ham, sipping white wine. It was 10.30 am. What a wonderful breakfast, in a city that starts dinner at 10 pm.

That day, lunch (at 3 pm) was a seafood soup which might have been called a *sarsuela*, but reminded me of the seafood soups of my childhood. After siesta, we emerged from the hotel for an *aperitivo* and a few snacks on sticks at a *pintxos* bar before our late dinner at the docks area called La Barceloneta, and our first try of paella and later *crèma Catalana* and xurros.

Catalan cuisine is rustic and rich in its variety of dishes, usually enhanced by the fundamental sauces and condiments: sofregit, picada, allioli and romesco. This is a cuisine that uses a lot of onions, garlic, capsicums (bell peppers), tomatoes, and hot spices such as paprika and cayenne pepper. The heat and intensity works very well. And they are not afraid to mix seafood with meats in their *Mar i muntanya*, confirming what a famous Catalan writer once said: 'The cuisine of a region is its landscape on a plate.'

PROVENCE

In Marseille, the 'real' bouillabaisse is served in two courses: a fish broth with crostini topped with rouille, and then the poached fish, enjoyed with a glass or two of the Provence rosé. But you don't need to do The Full Bouilly. Many restaurants, even tourist ones, offer an excellent fish soup — the bouillon of the bouillabaisse — still with crostini and rouille.

The market at the Old Port is like a village market inside a big city, where the fishermen sell their catch directly to the public for the best freshness and price.

Our greatest discovery was a simple restaurant called Toinou Les Fruits de Mer that has a fish market just outside, with beautiful seafood. You go there, choose your fish and seafood, then go inside and tell them the way you want it cooked, order a bottle of wine, sit down and it will be served to you. How civilised.

Ligurian cuisine is harmonious, nothing is overpowering ...

a green cuisine, simple, perfumed, subtle in the combination

of flavours, unified in the result that appears in front of you.

Between Marseille and Nice is St-Paul-de-Vence, often called the most beautiful village in the world. Many artisans and painters live here, and for decades they have been customers of La Colombe d'Or. Poets, writers and actors as well as artists such as Picasso, Miro, Renoir, Matisse, Giacometti and Chagal used to meet here in the summer, eating, playing and exchanging thoughts. Hanging on the walls of this incredible place are the best works of the best artists of the early 1900s. I'd like to think some people find similar stimulation in my restaurant in Sydney, where the walls are lined with the work of great Australian artists.

It seemed to me the Provençal table is very similar to the Ligurian table — bread, olive oil, olives, all the aromas of the garlic and herbs, fresh seafood, anchovies and, because of their glorious sun, a superb selection of vegetables. They can legitimately claim the title *La cuisine du soleil*. For me, the key difference between Provençal cuisine and Ligurian is in their use of mayonnaise and mustards to enhance the flavour and texture of their dishes.

LIGURIA

Genoa is the capital of Liguria, right in the middle of the arch that divides the region into two rivieras: *di Levante* (rising sun) and *di Ponente* (setting sun). Here is the real Mediterranean cuisine: poor, created by peasants, mountain people, sailors and fishermen. It is a cuisine that exalts the wild herbs, the basil, the seasonal vegetables, mushrooms, and the local seafood, all kept together by the olive oil — the gold of Liguria. While the Catalans love their almonds, the major nuts in Ligurian cooking are walnuts and pine nuts. According to legend, ravioli was invented in Liguria, to recycle chopped leftovers as a filling, and my preferred dressing for ravioli is the golden *salsa di noci* (walnut sauce). Pine nuts, never toasted, are for the pesto, of course, not only to dress pasta but also to flavour minestrone.

Ligurian cuisine is harmonious: all the ingredients are given a fair go, nothing is overpowering. This is a green cuisine, simple, perfumed, subtle in the combination of flavours, unified in the result that appears in front of you.

It's been a delight to explore two neighbouring cuisines that are tantalisingly different from my own, but equally true to their culture, history and traditions. If you cook everything in this book, you may conclude that all three are manifestations of one basic principle: the best cuisine in the world is the cooking you share with others.

— Lucio Galletto

Index

Thank you

Our profound thanks go to two genius chefs: Nicole Bampton and Janni Kyritsis. Nicole, executive chef at Lucio's restaurant, added precision to our vagueness, particularly with the dessert chapter, and produced dishes for the photo shoot that were as elegant to the eye as to the palate. Janni, after 40 years cooking in three-star restaurants, gave us the benefit of his library, his wisdom and, for one day, his hands (on the focaccia, the *pissaladiera* and the *coca*). We must also thank:

Ace photographer Bree Hutchins, who captured the countryside and the cooking.

The perfect fellow-travellers Fiona Williams and Victoria and Michael Greene, who opened our eyes to the Costa Brava (even if David missed the ladies of the highway). And Michael's mother Maria, his father (also called Michael) and his aunty Maria Teresa Mitjavila Cors, who helped us understand Catalan thinking.

Mario Guelfi, of Capannina Ciccio, for the hospitality and the helicopter.

Damien Pignolet, of Regatta restaurant and illustrious history, for his advice on the bouillabaisse and the loan of the *daubière*.

Matteo Galletto and Michele Rispoli, of Capriccio Osteria, who gave us the use of their ovens and their formula for the finest focaccia.

Paolo Calcagno, for the use of his basil farm near Prà.

Alexia Paoletti, merci pour Cassis, Le Rhul et Les Calanques.

Susan Williams, who began the selection process for our recipes, and offered essential encouragement.

Sally Galletto, who organised Lucio.

And the team at Murdoch Books, who made it all sensible and beautiful: publishing director Sue Hines, Diana Hill, Megan Pigott, Emma Hutchinson, Katri Hilden and Michelle Noerianto.

These books guided our travels, our cooking and our thinking:

The Food of France, Waverley Root (Alfred A. Knopf)

The Food of Italy, Waverley Root (Vintage Books)

Catalan Cuisine, Colman Andrews (The Harvard Common Press)

Flavours of the Riviera, Colman Andrews (Grub Street)

Cuisinière Catalane, Sonia Ezgulian (Les Cuisinières)

A Book of Mediterranean Food, Elizabeth David (Penguin)

The Mediterranean in History, David Abulafia (Thames & Hudson)

Mediterranean Cookery, Claudia Roden (Penguin)

Mediterranean Cooking, Paula Wolfert (The Ecco Press)

Spain: The Green Guide (Michelin)

Delizia! The Epic History of the Italians and Their Food, John Dickie (Sceptre)

La Cucina Ligure di Levante, Salvatore Marchese (Franco Muzzio Editore)

Honey from a Weed, Patience Gray (Harper & Row)

Cucina di Strettissimo Magro, P. S. Delle Piane (Il Golfo)

This edition published in 2021
Originally published in 2017 by Murdoch Books, an imprint of Allen & Unwin

Murdoch Books Australia
83 Alexander Street
Crows Nest NSW 2065
Phone: +61 (0) 2 8425 0100
Fax: +61 (0) 2 9906 2218
murdochbooks.com.au
info@murdochbooks.com.au

Murdoch Books UK
Ormond House
26–27 Boswell Street
London WC1N 3JZ
Phone: +44 (0) 20 8785 5995
murdochbooks.co.uk
info@murdochbooks.co.uk

For Corporate Orders & Custom Publishing, contact our Business Development Team
at salesenquiries@murdochbooks.com.au.

Publisher: Diana Hill
Editorial Manager: Emma Hutchinson
Design Manager and Cover Designer: Megan Pigott
Project Editor: Katri Hilden
Internal Designers: Northwood Green
Photographer: Bree Hutchins
Stylist: Michelle Noerianto
Production Manager: Rachel Walsh

A catalogue record for this
book is available from the
National Library of Australia

ISBN 978 1 92235 110 4 Australia
ISBN 978 1 91163 299 3 UK

A catalogue record for this book is available from the British Library.

Colour reproduction by Splitting Image Colour Studio Pty Ltd, Clayton, Victoria
Printed in China by C&C offset Printing Co., Ltd.

IMPORTANT: Those who might be at risk from the effects of salmonella poisoning (the elderly,
pregnant women, young children and those suffering from immune deficiency diseases) should
consult their doctor with any concerns about eating raw eggs.

OVEN GUIDE: You may find cooking times vary depending on the oven you are using. For fan-forced
ovens, as a general rule, set the oven temperature to 20°C (70°F) lower than indicated in the recipe.

MEASURES GUIDE: We have used 20 ml (4 teaspoon) tablespoon measures. If you are using a 15 ml
(3 teaspoon) tablespoon add an extra teaspoon of the ingredient for each tablespoon specified.

The paper in this book is FSC® certified.
FSC® promotes environmentally responsible,
socially beneficial and economically viable
management of the world's forests.